WHAT YOUR COLLEAGUES ARE SA'

Smashes the "born to teach" mythology. Instructional coaches and leaders, put this on your required reading list. You will reflect and be challenged on who you are as a teacher, and learn how to better understand those you work with. You will examine your own collaborative practices with colleagues, and will build your credibility with teachers and teacher credibility with students. Most important, learn what you can do to refine your credibility and strengthen your collective efficacy.

—Alison Venter
Education Consultant
Independent Schools Tasmania

There is so much that I love about this book! Fisher, Frey, and Smith have brought together their collective wisdom around learning and delivered it in a way that is research based and practical. This book not only makes me want to be a better facilitator of learning, it provides me with strong ideas of how to do it.

—Peter DeWitt
Consultant, Author
Instructional Leadership: Creating Practice Out of Theory
and *Coach It Further: Using the Art of Coaching*
to Improve School Leadership

The authors provide a compelling argument for the powerful influence that teacher credibility and collective efficacy have on the learning of both teachers and students. The concrete examples and tools map out effective actions teachers can use to integrate both teacher credibility and collective efficacy into their own practice.

—Amy Colton
Educational Consultant
Learning Forward Michigan

This book is both powerful and extremely practical. It fits perfectly with something I've been wrestling with a lot lately as a principal with way too many things on my plate. This project is the intersection of two high-leverage things we can control and improve upon: building the capacity of both teams and individual teachers, resulting in higher levels of learning for the kids that we serve. The great thing about how the authors laid this out? (1) It promotes solid self-reflection throughout the book, and (2) it offers strategies and ideas that will be fairly easy for our teachers and our staff as a whole to "try on."

—Brett Wille
Hidden River Middle School

After reading *The Teacher Credibility and Collective Efficacy Playbook,* I'm excited to take steps with new teachers to support them in understanding the impact of building relationships and credibility with their students from the get-go. Supporting teacher teams in order to take their work to the next level is the work of our county office. Those who have the direct access to students are the ones who have the most impact on them! Working together can and will make a difference in our students' lives.

—Cathy Cranson
Director of Special Projects
Monterey County Office of Education

THE TEACHER CREDIBILITY AND COLLECTIVE EFFICACY PLAYBOOK

GRADES K-12

THE TEACHER CREDIBILITY AND COLLECTIVE EFFICACY PLAYBOOK

GRADES K-12

Douglas Fisher

Nancy Frey

Dominique Smith

Foreword by John Hattie

CORWIN

Fisher & Frey

FOR INFORMATION:

Corwin

A SAGE Company

2455 Teller Road

Thousand Oaks, California 91320

(800) 233-9936

www.corwin.com

SAGE Publications Ltd.

1 Oliver's Yard

55 City Road

London EC1Y 1SP

United Kingdom

SAGE Publications India Pvt. Ltd.

B 1/I 1 Mohan Cooperative Industrial Area

Mathura Road, New Delhi 110 044

India

SAGE Publications Asia-Pacific Pte. Ltd.

18 Cross Street #10-10/11/12

China Square Central

Singapore 048423

Director and Publisher, Corwin Classroom: Lisa Luedeke

Editorial Development Manager: Julie Nemer

Associate Content Development Editor: Sharon Wu

Project Editor: Amy Schroller

Copy Editor: Cate Huisman

Typesetter: C&M Digitals (P) Ltd.

Proofreader: Susan Schon

Indexer: Judy Hunt

Cover and Interior Designer: Rose Storey

Marketing Manager: Deena Meyer

Printed in the United States of America

ISBN 978-1- 0718-1254- 9

This book is printed on acid-free paper.

20 21 22 23 24 10 9 8 7 6 5 4 3 2 1

CONTENTS

Visit the companion website at
resources.corwin.com/teachercredibilityplaybook
to view the provided videos.

LIST OF VIDEOS

FOREWORD

When we asked over 600 adults to recall their best teachers and say why these teachers were best, the answers did not include *because she taught me music or math, because he was fun and knew so much, because she was nice and liked me,* or *because he let me choose what I wanted to do and taught me to listen carefully.* No, the answers generally showed that the teachers turned the students on to their passion, or they saw something in students that students did not see in themselves. An ability to build confidence to exceed one's expectations, and to turn on the excitement and passion of learning, makes a teacher great. Teachers who can make this happen have high credibility, and we need many more of them.

It is probably no different in the staff room—those leaders who turn others on to the passion of learning, who maximize impact, and who have social sensitivity to empathize where others are coming from and how they are thinking and feeling—these are the leaders who make a difference in teachers' lives as well. This book brings together two of the most powerful notions in teaching—teacher credibility and collective efficacy—two that combine in a powerful recipe for truly enhancing impact on student learning.

Now consider asking students (or teachers) before they walk into a classroom (or staffroom)—do you think you are going to learn something from this teacher (this school leader)? If they say no, then it is highly likely they will learn little—because of this belief, and not necessarily related to what the teacher (or school leader) does. Building credibility that the teacher (or leader) can make the difference, can turn students on to their passion, and is able to see potential beyond what the student sees—is the core notion. And as is true with many such notions (e.g., trust, confidence, fairness), we do not need to wait to build confidence and credibility: It can happen very quickly—from Day 1.

We can show that we are credible by demonstrating that we have social sensitivity, can listen, and can turn students on to their passion of learning. Also, we can turn it off as quickly, especially through sarcasm, ignoring a student, making students "do" too much and not be challenged, showing low empathy, and not having deep content knowledge to stretch and excite.

Fisher, Frey, and Smith outline the major components of credibility: Is the teacher believable, convincing, and capable of persuading students that they can be successful? Does the teacher engender high trust, competence, dynamism, and immediacy? They also outline the main features of collective efficacy—when a group of people exceeds what each can bring to the task, each believing that everyone can contribute, and all having a high level of confidence that they can very positively impact the learning of all students in the school.

If only implementing these two core notions were easy.

There are many recommendations throughout this book. While most are practical and can be observed, the underlying notions are ways of thinking. They are about becoming a teacher who knows how students are thinking, how they are solving problems, their levels of confidence, their beliefs about the teacher, and their expectations about success. As important is how students react to failure—do they see errors as opportunities, are they prepared to fight back when not successful, do they see more wisdom in a group than preferring to sit and work alone? Students "know" when teachers know this kind of information—and it is the essence of credibility.

The notions of teacher credibility and collective efficacy are rich in research history. And as always it is the fidelity, dosage, adaptability, and quality of implementation of these ideas in your class and school that matter.

—John Hattie
Author, *Visible Learning,* and
Director of the Melbourne Education Research Institute
University of Melbourne, Australia

ACKNOWLEDGMENTS

Corwin gratefully acknowledges the contributions of the following reviewers:

Amy Colton
Education Consultant
Learning Forward Michigan
Ann Arbor, MI

Peter DeWitt
Author and Consultant
Albany, NY

Sonja Hollins-Alexander
Director of Professional Learning
Corwin
Thousand Oaks, CA

John Scovill
Principal
Pioneer Elementary School
Preston, ID

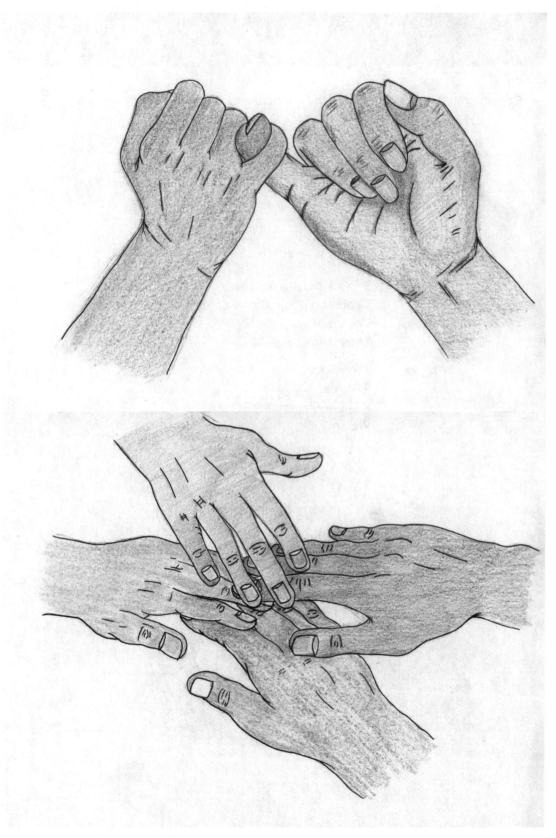

Artwork by high school student Jesus Sanchez

INTRODUCTION

LINKING TEACHER CREDIBILITY AND COLLECTIVE EFFICACY

This book is about **you**, and it is for **you**. This is not a book of teaching strategies, although there are strategies included in it. Rather, it is a book about the actions you can take to increase your credibility with students as well as your collective efficacy as a member of your school team. When you increase your credibility with your students, they learn more. And when you increase your collective efficacy, they learn even faster. We were motivated to write this book because there is a powerful synergy between teacher credibility and collective efficacy. These two ideas are among the strongest influences on student achievement. Hattie (2018) collected meta-analyses, or studies of studies of influences on student achievement, from all over the world. At this point, his database represents over 300 million students. As quantified by Hattie, the average effect of an influence is .40, and as you will see, teacher credibility and collective efficacy are well above average. However, these relational elements of our profession are rarely mined with intention. Instead, we seem to be governed by folk wisdom about what we do in the company of students and colleagues.

Together We Are Stronger

ENTER AND OBSERVE the sights and sounds of a school that has embraced teacher credibility and collective efficacy.

TEACHER CREDIBILITY

Let's start with teacher credibility, which is students' perceptions of their teacher's competence, dynamism, trustworthiness, and immediacy (McCroskey & Young, 1981). A student's ability to learn is influenced by whether the source (the teacher) is believed to be knowledgeable (competent), enthusiastic (dynamic), reliable (trustworthy), and accessible (immediate). In other words, learning isn't purely a cognitive function. It is governed by the social and emotional perceptions that lie just below the surface.

REFLECTIVE WRITING

What might be the long-term implications of teachers having low credibility with students?

We have seen too many teachers implement what should have been effective instructional strategies, but not get the impact they hoped for. You've heard that learning is a social endeavor? Teacher credibility is part of the social nature of learning.

Teacher credibility is sometimes confused with the concept of authority. Being authoritarian does not build credibility. And simply asserting yourself as an authority will not ensure that students learn at high levels. We've all met people who clearly are experts, authorities as it were, in an area. But if we did not trust them, if they were not dynamic and willing to share, and if we did not feel a connection with them, we probably did not give them much of our attention and may even have disregarded what they said. The medical field calls this bedside manner; in education, it is called teacher credibility.

We want to be sure to avoid a false dichotomy here. There isn't a binary credible/noncredible teacher. We are all on a continuum with our students. Our actions are always observed and judged by students, and our credibility quotient is updated continually. Of course, the more credit you have with a given student, the easier it is to repair a problematic interaction. Effective teachers build their credits with students so that there is some wiggle room when missteps by either party occur.

> Teacher credibility is students' belief that they can learn from a particular teacher, because this adult is believable, convincing, and capable of persuading students that they can be successful. Students are very perceptive about which teachers can make a difference for them.

REFLECTIVE WRITING

Based on this introduction, how credible are you with students?

COLLECTIVE TEACHER EFFICACY

Collective teacher efficacy refers to a staff's shared belief that through their collective action, they can positively influence student outcomes, including for students who are disengaged and/or disadvantaged.

Collective teacher efficacy is the belief of a group that they possess the wherewithal to positively impact student learning. Members of a group with a high degree of collective efficacy have confidence that they can successfully execute a course of action (Bandura, 1997). Evidence of collective efficacy transcends professions. Athletes draw on their beliefs about the success of their team to win the game. Military forces count on their beliefs that fellow soldiers are providing top-notch information and making wise decisions. To return to the medical field, patients under the care of nurses with a high degree of collective efficacy heal more rapidly. There is an interaction between teacher credibility and collective teacher efficacy. These two constructs can either undermine or amplify our efforts.

REFLECTIVE WRITING

How much does your team reflect the values of collective efficacy?

WHEN TEACHER CREDIBILITY AND COLLECTIVE EFFICACY COLLIDE

Marc Kilpatrick distributes a text to his fourth graders, and says, "We're reading this text today. I'm not sure that you'll understand it but give it a try." He does not let the students know the purpose of the lesson or even that they will be reading about animal adaptation (something most nine-year-olds think is pretty cool). He quickly informs students about the process of reciprocal teaching, which they have never done before, and then tells them it is time to start. Brittany does not start right away; she's talking with a peer rather than reading. Mr. Kilpatrick interrupts the task, saying, "Brittany, move your clip. You should be reading, not talking." Brittany leaves her chair and walks to the board. She moves the clothespin with her name on it from green to yellow, indicating that she now has a warning for behavior and next will be sent to the principal.

So much has happened in these few minutes, and each of the teacher's actions has the potential to accelerate or prevent learning. On the one hand, Mr. Kilpatrick is using an evidence-based instructional routine. Reciprocal teaching has four decades' worth of research demonstrating its above-average impact ("250+ Influences," n.d.). On the other hand, the strategy will probably not compensate for the lack of teacher credibility. Mr. Kilpatrick does not seem excited or passionate about the lesson. He fails to invite students into the learning and doesn't even let them know what they are learning or why it is relevant. He does not convey optimism or even an expectation that they will be successful. He doesn't fully explain the task, leaving several students confused about what to do next. And he uses public humiliation as a classroom management tool, allowing students to wonder if he even cares about them. The odds are that Mr. Kilpatrick's students are not going to learn at high levels, even though he is using an otherwise effective instructional approach.

But his lack of credibility with students spills over into his work with colleagues. Mr. Kilpatrick was doubtful when his grade-level chair, Marsha Findlay, discussed reciprocal teaching a few weeks ago. She shared the many benefits of the strategy but didn't spend much time on the details. Ms. Findlay prepared some handouts explaining the process. However, the team didn't discuss a plan for building their students' capacity to take on this complex technique. Further, these fourth-grade teachers don't have a shared expectation of spending time in each other's classrooms, so they rarely discuss instructional practices. Another colleague, Bob Santana, has used reciprocal teaching for several years and is a master at it. But no one else knows that, and Mr. Santana certainly isn't going to volunteer that information for fear of being seen as the know-it-all. He's concerned that sharing his success seems like bragging. Besides, Mr. Santana knows that there are more parent complaints about Mr. Kilpatrick than any other teacher in the school, and more requests to transfer students out of his class. *It's not my job to fix that*, he thinks to himself. *I just need to take care of my students. Maybe the principal will get fed up and do something about it.*

REFLECTIVE WRITING

How might teachers new to the school or grade level feel when they are not able to collaborate with their peers on curriculum, instruction, and assessment?

WHEN TEACHER CREDIBILITY AND COLLECTIVE EFFICACY THRIVE

Fourth-grade teacher Arnold Schmidt works at a neighboring elementary school in the same district as Mr. Kilpatrick and his colleagues. Mr. Schmidt is knowledgeable about the influence of teacher credibility on student learning and is therefore intentional about his practice. Mr. Schmidt holds up a book and talks about it. He's giving an overview, hoping that some students will want to read this particular book on their own. As is consistent with the research (e.g., Marinak & Gambrell, 2016), he does this every day with several books. He selects texts that he believes will appeal to his students and usually manages to strike a chord, because he pays attention to their interests and aspirations. The book he has in his hand is about computer coding, something several students have grown interested in due to an afterschool video club they've joined. Mr. Schmidt is enthusiastic, saying, "I hope someone decides to read this and then teach me some things about coding! This didn't exist when I was in school."

When one table of students starts talking to each other, the teacher says, "I'm glad to hear you're excited about this topic. Let's chat about this when we're walking to lunch. I'd like to hear what you are thinking about."

Fellow teacher Yasmin Jackson is taking notes in the back of the classroom. Members of her grade-level team are regularly in and out of each other's classroom, to the point where some students will say they have five teachers, not just one. Their team decided the previous week to revisit book talks. "We were all feeling like we were stuck in a rut," said Ms. Jackson. In advance of their next meeting, they are each watching one another during book talks. They'll discuss at their upcoming meeting their observations and what students told them about the practice. Getting student feedback in classrooms other than their own is natural, because the children know all the fourth-grade teachers well.

"This is how we cross-pollinate ideas," said Mr. Schmidt.

"It's amazing to watch how ideas bloom when we're together," Ms. Jackson noted.

NOTES

THE LONG-TERM IMPLICATIONS OF TEACHER CREDIBILITY AND COLLECTIVE EFFICACY

Mr. Kilpatrick had low expectations for his students, and his team might have supported him to have higher expectations for students. Unfortunately, Mr. Kilpatrick works at a school in which teachers are lone rangers. They do have grade-level meetings, but these conversations are operational in nature. Teachers rarely talk about curriculum, instruction, or assessment in detail. They don't examine student work or look at the relationship between their impact and student support needs. These dispositions are cultivated by a school culture that values competition over collaboration.

As the school year drew to a close, the teachers at Mr. Kilpatrick's school were given cards with students' names on them. They were asked to put colored sticky dots on the back of each card to indicate the following:

- English learner
- Student with a disability
- Difficult parent
- Behavior problems
- Gifted/talented
- Attendance problems
- Low test scores

The team received their cards from their third-grade colleagues. They then had what they call a "card party," in which they formed the classes for the following year. The principal said it was for the purpose of "balancing classes." But our observation was that there was a lot of trading between teachers. In fact, it more closely resembled a fantasy football draft than a careful consideration of student strengths and needs.

Mr. Kilpatrick said, "I've had a rough year and I deserve a few more GATE students, but I'm okay with more difficult parents."

Upon hearing that remark, Mr. Santana thought to himself, *No, you're actually not. But if you want to believe that, fine by me.*

To our thinking, this is not building the collective efficacy of the group and does not ensure that teachers have high expectations for all their students or each other as professionals. In this case, an entrenched system perpetuates an inequitable distribution of resources and diminishes the potential collective efficacy of the organization.

At the school where Yasmin Jackson and Bob Findlay teach, preparations are underway for building next year's classes. Teachers completed summaries of each student and submitted them to the principal, Elena Flint. The teachers are asked to comment on the social, emotional, and academic needs of their current students, not on demographics. "We have a computer to do that," she says. The school management information system creates draft class lists for the following year such that students are placed randomly in classes. The principal reviews the computer-generated lists to ensure that classes are balanced and that each student's needs can be met based on her teachers' credibility with students.

Ms. Flint meets with each grade-level team to discuss her proposed lists, and she brokers changes personally. "We don't 'trade' children. This isn't a swap meet," she said later. "Our focus as a school, and with each team, is on how we can create the best ecosystem we can to support the needs of every student."

Ms. Jackson, who is finishing her third year of teaching, is feeling confident about her ability to address the needs and strengths of next year's students. "Look at the team I've got around me," she said. "These people are my best resources. I know here I don't ever have to sit with a dilemma all by myself."

NOTES

A CHAIN IS AS STRONG AS ITS WEAKEST LINK

There is an adage that states that a chain is only as strong as its weakest link. The relative strength of a team—its collective efficacy—erodes when a member struggles and yet does not receive support. The damage done when a member leaves the school, district, or profession because of low credibility with students persists long after the departure. In fact, the only thing it does strengthen is the belief that each member is on his or her own to sink or swim.

REFLECTIVE WRITING

How do you see these two ideas, teacher credibility and collective teacher efficacy, fitting together?

THE ORGANIZATION OF THIS BOOK

The first part of this book addresses teacher credibility and focuses on specific actions you can take to increase your credibility with students. Teacher credibility is an individual score. And it's an important factor that has been underrecognized in school improvement efforts. But students' learning is also influenced by the collective efficacy of their teachers. Individual efforts are important, and so are collective efforts. Thus, we spend the second half of this book focused on collective efficacy. We review the components of collective teacher efficacy, which also has an above-average impact on students' learning ("250+ Influences," n.d.).

We believe that teacher credibility and collective efficacy are important considerations for school improvement and student learning. And we think that they need to be combined and addressed simultaneously. If teacher credibility is high with some staff but they are not engaged in a collective, they are likely to burn out. And, it's hard to build collective efficacy when teachers are not credible with their students. Both are necessary. And both are within reach.

Each chapter starts with an introductory video in which Doug outlines some of the concepts. In addition, each chapter includes several videos in which Dominique shares his thinking and experiences. We call this feature a Think Along, as we hope you'll consider the ideas Dominique shares and think along with him as he talks. Each chapter concludes with a challenge. In these videos, Nancy provides a summarizing challenge for the chapter that will build your credibility or collective efficacy.

In addition, each chapter includes several Reflective Writing prompts in the margins of the text that allow you to record your thinking as you read. Further, there are Pause & Ponder tasks in which you will assess the skills and data collection tools that allow you to obtain information from students and/or your colleagues. We hope that these features allow you to engage with our ideas and continue to grow as a professional. As one of our colleagues often says, "You don't have to be sick to get better." The same applies to teaching and learning: We can all get better. Focusing on your credibility and collective efficacy are two ways that you continue to grow as a professional. We hope you enjoy the process.

TEACHER & COLLECTIVE
CREDIBILITY EFFICACY

noun | cred·i·bil·i·ty |
\ ˌkre-də-ˈbi-lə-tē \

The quality or power of
inspiring belief

noun | ef·fi·ca·cy |
\ ˈe-fi-kə-sē \

The power to produce an effect

WHAT STUDENTS REMEMBER

Teacher credibility and collective efficacy are powerful tools that can accelerate students' learning. Importantly, they are always in play even if we don't attend to them. When we neglect these two concepts, learning suffers. When we embrace them, our professional lives are improved, and our students learn more.

At some point in your career, a student will return and ask you the question that every amazing teacher has been asked since time immemorial: "Do you remember me?" When that happens, you'll remember the rows upon rows of students you have taught and how this one who has returned impacted your life. Students remember their teachers, especially the ones who exhibited care, compassion, high expectations, and support. And not only do they remember those amazing teachers, they learn more from them.

Dominique remembers a particular science teacher. She was passionate about science, even if Dominique wasn't at the time. She developed amazing relationships with students, knew everyone's names, and knew what each was interested in. She often asked Dominique about his performance at the football game and even showed up during playoffs to cheer Dominique and his teammates on. It seemed as though all of the students trusted her and felt a special connection with her. She was compassionate and kind, and yet she held high expectations for her students.

Dominique recalls two incidents that solidified her reputation with him as a credible teacher. First, there was a student with a physical disability in Dominique's class. This student had a hard time sitting on the lab stools without falling off. The special education staff thought he could remain in his wheelchair, but the teacher was concerned that he would not be able to participate in group work. The teacher asked the students to problem-solve the situation and come prepared to share their ideas. This was not part of the official curriculum of the class, but rather an expectation of the classroom community for students to take care of each other. The following week, as asked, groups of students proposed ways to address the situation so that their peer could join them at the lab bench. Dominique's group proposed to have one of the labs lowered so that his group could collaborate. As he remembers, "My buddy Jeff said that we could just cut the legs off of one of the tables and make it the right size." The class decided to go with another idea, namely that they would take a dining room chair with arms and cut off the legs of that chair and bolt it to the lab stool. The teacher said that she would check with the students' parents and the principal. A few days later, a chair modified as the group had suggested appeared, and the problem was solved.

Introducing Teacher Credibility and Collective Efficacy.

LISTEN as Doug introduces the idea of teacher credibility and collective efficacy.

REFLECTIVE WRITING

Dominique's science teacher never gave up on him or let him give up on himself. What did this teacher do to build her credibility?

_____

_____

_____

_____

_____

_____

_____

_____

_____

A second example of the credibility of this science teacher was more personal for Dominique. Several weeks into the class, he failed a test. He had failed tests in other classes before, but the averages always seemed to work in his favor, and he passed his classes. At the time, he was more interested in athletics than academics, but he did well enough in his courses. When he failed that science test, something different happened. The teacher met with him and reviewed each incorrect answer. She told him that for each of his incorrect answers, he needed to write a description of his thinking at the time. _What misconceptions or confusions had led him to the answer he selected? What new information showed him why that could not be the right answer?_

He remembers her saying, "Why don't you just do two of these tonight? I know you have practice today, so let's just start with two of them. I'll check with your coach to make sure you have a little time."

He did as she asked and then was given more to do each day. At one point, the teacher told Dominique that he was ready to retake the test. In reflecting on this, Dominique says, "I stood there in shock. I had never been allowed to take a test again. It was clear that she expected that I would learn this science and that I would show her that I learned it. So, I took the test and earned a nearly perfect score." When she handed the test back to him privately, the teacher said, "We can do this for every test this year. I just want you to learn. It doesn't matter to me how long it takes. I'm here for you." He found out later that she did this with every student who initially failed a test. Parenthetically, Dominique earned an A in the class and ended up taking several more advanced science classes, because this teacher ignited a passion in him. In essence, she invited him into his own education.

PAUSE & PONDER

Take a moment and reflect on who you are as an educator and what your role means to you. In the spaces below, capture words, phrases, and pictures that recognize the "plus" about who you are as a teacher.

Why did you become
an educator?

What makes you a
great teacher?

What is your hope
for your students?

What goals do you
have for yourself as
an educator?

TEACHER CREDIBILITY DEFINED

Researchers have examined the dynamic affective moves of the teacher and identified the actions and dispositions they exhibit. In the research world, this construct is known as teacher credibility. Teacher credibility has a strong effect size at 1.09, well above the average impact of .40 ("250+ Influences," n.d.). To put it in perspective, teacher credibility has twice as much influence on achievement as does student motivation, and twice the impact of socioeconomic status. That's powerful and worth further exploration.

At the basic level, teacher credibility is students' perception that they will learn from this adult. The adult is seen as believable, convincing, and capable of persuading students that they can be successful. Students know which teachers can make a difference, and this can fluctuate. As we have previously noted, "The dynamic of teacher credibility is *always* at play" (Fisher, Frey, & Hattie, 2016, p. 10). We point out in our introduction that there are four components of teacher credibility outlined in the research: trust, competence, dynamism, and immediacy. Thankfully, there are specific actions that teachers can take to increase their credibility in each of these areas.

THINK ALONG

Trust. Dominique discusses trust and the value of trust in schools. How much trust exists in your classroom? Are there ways that you can build trust?

Trust

Students need to know that their teachers really care about them as individuals and have their best academic and social interests at heart. Students also want to know that their teachers are true to their word and are reliable. A few points about trust:

1. If you make a promise, work to keep it (or explain why you could not).

2. Tell students the truth about their performance. (They know when their work is below standard and wonder why you are telling them otherwise.)

3. Don't spend all of your time trying to catch students in the wrong (and yet be honest about the impact that their behavior has on you as an individual).

4. Examine any negative feelings you have about specific students. (They sense it, and it compromises the trust within the classroom.)

Competence

In addition to trust, students want to know that their teachers know their stuff and know how to teach that stuff. They expect an appropriate level of expertise and accuracy from their teachers. Further, students measure competence by the ability of the teacher to deliver instruction that is coherent and organized. They expect that lessons are well paced and include accurate information.

1. Make sure you know the content well, and be honest when a question arises that you are not sure about. (This requires planning in advance.)

2. Organize lesson delivery in a cohesive and coherent way.

3. Consider your nonverbal behaviors that communicate competence, such as the position of your hands when you talk with students or the facial expressions you make. (Students notice defensive positions, and they recognize nonverbal indications that they are not valued when they speak.)

TEACHER CREDIBILITY HAS TWICE AS MUCH INFLUENCE ON ACHIEVEMENT AS DOES STUDENT MOTIVATION, AND TWICE THE IMPACT OF SOCIOECONOMIC STATUS.

Dynamism

This dimension of teacher credibility focuses on the passion teachers bring to the classroom and their content. It is really about the ability to communicate your enthusiasm for your subject and your students. And it's about developing spirited lessons that capture students' interest. To improve dynamism, consider the following:

1. Rekindle your passion for the content you teach by focusing on the aspects that got you excited as a student. Remember why you wanted to be a teacher and the content you wanted to introduce to your students. Students notice when their teachers are bored by the content and when

their teachers aren't really interested in the topic. We think that a teacher's motto should be, Make content interesting!

2. Consider the relevance of your lessons. Does the content lend itself to application outside the classroom? Do students have opportunities to learn about themselves and their problem solving? Does the content help them become civic minded and engaged in the community? Does it connect to universal human experiences or ask students to grapple with ethical concerns? When there isn't relevance, students check out and may be compliant learners rather than committed learners.

3. Seek feedback from trusted colleagues about your lesson delivery. Ask peers to focus on the energy you bring to the lessons and the impact of those lessons, rather than on the individual instructional strategies you use. Students respond to the passion and energy in a lesson, even if they don't initially think they will be interested.

INSIDE THE CLASSROOM

Watch a kindergarten teacher work with her students. In what ways does she enact the principles of teacher credibility?

Immediacy

This final construct of teacher credibility focuses on *accessibility* and *relatability* as perceived by students. Teachers who move around the room and are easy to interact with increase students' perception of immediacy.

Teachers need to be accessible, and yet there needs to be a sense of urgency— this signals to students that their learning is important.

1. Get to know something personal about each student, as students know when you don't know their names or anything about them.

2. Teach with urgency but not to the point that it causes undue stress for them. That said, students want to know that their learning matters and that you are not wasting their time.

3. Start the class on time, and use every minute wisely. This means that there are tasks students can complete while you engage in routine tasks, such as taking attendance, and that you have a series of sponge activities ready when lessons run short. Students notice when time is wasted. And when there is "free time," they believe that their learning is not an urgent consideration of their teachers.

When a teacher is *not* perceived as credible, students tune out. And quite frankly, we can't afford for students to do so. We need them to engage, to trust their teachers, and to choose to participate in their learning. These four aspects of teacher credibility—trust, competence, dynamism, and immediacy—can help them do just that. But, as we noted in the introduction, we cannot stop at the individual level. The power of the collective cannot be forgotten.

When a teacher is *not* perceived as credible, students tune out.
iStock.com/fizkes

PAUSE & PONDER

Capture the essence of each of the characteristics of teacher credibility in 10 words or fewer, and record them in the graphic organizer below. Which of the four aspects of teacher credibility are highest for you? Which is an area of growth?

Say it in 10 words or less!

- Refer to pages 16–19 in this chapter that talk about each characteristic of teacher credibility.
- Capture the essence of each characteristic in ten words or less.

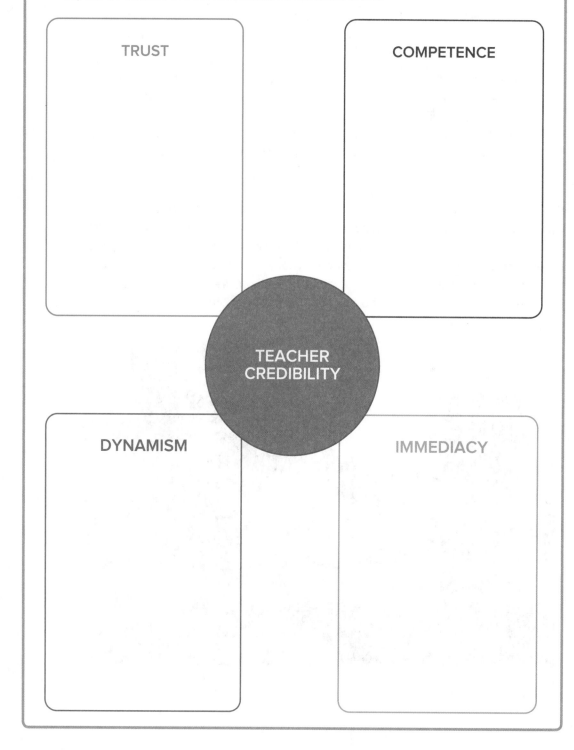

TRUST

COMPETENCE

TEACHER CREDIBILITY

DYNAMISM

IMMEDIACY

COLLECTIVE TEACHER EFFICACY

THINK ALONG

Collective Efficacy.
Dominique discusses collective efficacy. As he talks, think about your team. How well do you function? Do you believe that you have the power to significantly impact students' learning? Do you have the tools to do so?

The concept of collective efficacy was introduced by Bandura (1997), who defined it as "a group's shared belief in the conjoint capabilities to organize and execute the courses of action required to produce given levels of attainment" (p. 477). That's pretty technical, so we will take it apart. There is a group of people. And this group believes in the abilities of their group. And this group does what it takes to achieve their goal. Collective efficacy has been studied rather extensively in education, and there is strong evidence for its impact on students' learning. In addition, as Hoy, Sweetland, and Smith (2002) note, there is a reciprocal relationship between individual and collective efficacy. As one gets stronger, so does the other. Strong collective efficacy seems to encourage individual teachers to make more effective use of the skills they already have. And strong individual efficacy allows teams to function more productively. Interestingly, Hoy and colleagues (2002) noted that a higher degree of collective efficacy positively impacted the academic press of the school. In other words, teachers are more likely to hold higher academic expectations for students when a strong level of collective efficacy is also present.

Consider the interactions a team of middle school mathematics teachers had. They were focused on a particular standard that was a challenge the previous year. Floyd Daniels said, "I remember this one last year. We had to do a lot of reteaching, remember? We had a plan, but it just didn't work out at first. Maybe we need to rethink the plan for this year."

"You're so right," Debbie Birks responded. "But we got there with almost every student. Remember when we were trading students, and Gustavo [Carrera, a fellow teacher] took on some of the students who really struggled, and you [referencing Mr. Daniels] took a large group of students—I think it was about 55—who had the concepts, and you gave them more practice and some extension tasks?"

Mr. Daniels laughed, adding "Yeah, I didn't think I had it in me to teach a group that large, but you all convinced me, and it was a really good experience. We did good work. But what about this year?"

Mr. Carrera joins the conversation. "It was valuable last year to have some reteaching time for a few days with the students who were struggling. And it was valuable that those who had mastered it got some extension instruction at the same time. But let's see if we can prevent some of that need for remediation this year. I think we need to start over with this unit plan. Last year, I think we started well above what the students already knew. And some of the tasks were too obscure for them. We need to break it down right from the beginning. And then we can go fast, once we're sure they have the concepts."

"So is that our goal for this unit?" Mr. Daniels offered. "We want to reduce the amount of remediation we have to do?"

"I think that's part of it, but let's add to it." Mr. Carrera replied. "We want to increase the precision of our teaching in this unit, so that we can accelerate their learning." The others nodded. "That means we need to make our assessments work better for us," said Mr. Daniels.

INSIDE THE CLASSROOM

Watch a math teacher work with his students. In what ways does he display a high degree of efficacy?

"Let's take a look at an initial assessment so we can figure out what they know and don't know," Ms. Birks said. "Gustavo, how about if you and I collaborate and draft an initial assessment for the team to review and revise?"

"That would be great," said Mr. Daniels. "While you do that, I'll review our plan from last year to see where we can build in more incremental practice throughout to solidify their skills. We weren't doing practice tests with students at this time last year. But we've seen how well that has worked for us in the first quarter. Let's find out how deliberate practice and practice tests work for us in this unit. Debbie, I want to be sure to use the self-assessment tool you developed for the last unit."

"Let me grab the assessment binder from my classroom," Mr. Carrera added. "It's got a lot of resources in there for us to use."

The team engaged in their planning processes, confident that they would make a difference. There are several things we think are important about their efforts.

First, they believe that their students can learn and that they have the power to teach the students well. This is an important aspect of collective efficacy and one that is often forgotten. Despite last year's struggles, there was no retreat from the academic press of high expectations. Nor did they fall into the trap of blaming students. When teachers believe in themselves, their team, and their students, they are well on their way to ensuring learning.

Second, the team focused on impact. They knew the impact that they had, and they focused on their impact collectively. Spending time with people you like, talking about your expectations, may be fun, but unless there is evidence of impact, collective efficacy will be stifled. Teams thrive on success. They look for it and celebrate it. In doing so, they build and reinforce the collective.

Third, they analyzed what worked and what did not work.

They were honest with each other and had ideas about what to keep and what to change. They did not pretend everything worked and felt comfortable with acknowledging individual contributions to the collective. Their ideas flowed freely, and they worked collaboratively. And finally, they focused on action. They did not admire the problem; they acknowledged their challenges and focused on things that they could do to move learning forward.

STRONG COLLECTIVE EFFICACY ENCOURAGES INDIVIDUAL TEACHERS TO MAKE EFFECTIVE USE OF THE SKILLS THEY ALREADY HAVE. STRONG INDIVIDUAL EFFICACY ALLOWS TEAMS TO FUNCTION PRODUCTIVELY.

REFLECTIVE WRITING

How were the middle school math teachers' interactions similar to, or different from, those you have with your team?

The math team's willingness and ability to reexamine and improve their practices stems from their school's focus on two dimensions of collective teacher efficacy. The first is that they continually reinvest in the relational conditions within the team. Relational conditions describe the interactions and communication of the team, how they work through challenges, and how they learn from one another. The relational conditions of a team are always in play and require continual attention throughout, as they strongly influence the extent to which peers support peers. The second dimension of collective teacher efficacy is the collaborative action they take. Without collaborative action, the team will not move forward, and instead will stagnate. The math team's collaborative actions are derived from the research on goal attainment, organizational learning, and impact on student achievement.

Together, these two dimensions contribute to the collective efficacy of the team and result in what Hoy and colleagues call "the normative and behavioral environment of the school" (2002, p. 79). The components of this model are not strictly linear. Rather, they are essential habits for moving adult learning forward while building the relational strengths among professional colleagues to take on the work (see Figure 1.1).

THE INTERSECTION OF TEACHER CREDIBILITY AND COLLECTIVE EFFICACY

These two constructs do not exist in silos, separated by time and audience. While a teacher's credibility is a function of student perceptions, it is an open secret among the faculty. We all know who those highly credible teachers are in our buildings, even if we have never set foot in their classrooms. It is the band teacher who your students chatter about because they feel successful under her tutelage. The kindergarten teacher who your fifth graders still seek out, or the English teacher whose graduates stop by to visit years later. They aren't simply "popular"—there is substance behind what they accomplish with students.

Credibility is essential to the collective work of adult teams. We are appreciative of colleagues who possess expertise in the technical aspects of curriculum, instruction, and assessment. But teachers who are highly credible with their students are desirable to their teams, because we know they skillfully weave technical expertise with the social sensitivity needed to work with children and youth.

> THE SECOND DIMENSION OF COLLECTIVE TEACHER EFFICACY IS THE COLLABORATIVE ACTION THEY TAKE. WITHOUT COLLABORATIVE ACTION, THE TEAM WILL NOT MOVE FORWARD.

Figure 1.1 A model for collective efficacy and professional learning

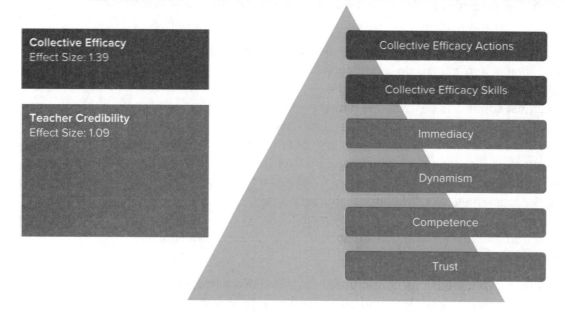

Collective Efficacy
Effect Size: 1.39

Teacher Credibility
Effect Size: 1.09

Collective Efficacy Actions

Collective Efficacy Skills

Immediacy

Dynamism

Competence

Trust

Now consider how credibility and collective efficacy conjoin. Those who contribute to the collective efficacy of the group are professionally generous, sharing insights while remaining open to new ideas. They are skilled at mediating the thinking of others, asking questions that expand, rather than shut down, conversation. They are trustworthy, maintaining confidences appropriately so that colleagues can be vulnerable. A group's dynamics are influenced by the credibility of its members, which in turn enhance or inhibit its collective efficacy. In the sections that follow, we describe the characteristics and dispositions of four types of team members and their potential impact (see Figure 1.2).

Those who contribute to the collective efficacy of the group are professionally generous.
iStock.com/fizkes

Figure 1.2 A matrix of teacher credibility and collective efficacy

"The Talker"	"The Amplifier"
Professionally generous with colleagues	Professionally generous with colleagues
Values the company of colleagues	Seeks to learn shoulder-to-shoulder with colleagues
Holds an optimistic view of colleagues and the school	Has an optimistic view of students, colleagues, and the school
Likes working with adults; tolerates students	Perceived by students as competent, trustworthy, dynamic, and caring
Rarely turns ideas into action or has impact	Perceived by colleagues as competent, trustworthy, dynamic, and accessible
Holds a pessimistic view of students and has low expectations for them	Students and colleagues reach their potential because of this person
Held in low regard by students	
High Collective Efficacy	*High Collective Efficacy*
Low Teacher Credibility	*High Teacher Credibility*

"The Loner"	"The Independent Contractor"
Is isolated socially and emotionally by colleagues	Isolates self socially and emotionally from colleagues
Practice is private and not shared	Practice is private, secretive, and not shared
Colleagues avoid engaging beyond necessary interactions	Has an optimistic view of students
Holds a pessimistic view of students, colleagues, and the school	Has a pessimistic view of colleagues and the school
Students are wary and avoid interacting beyond minimal compliance	Is not open to the ideas of others
Not held in high regard by students	Perceived by students as competent, trustworthy, dynamic, and accessible
Wonders whether this is the right profession for him or her	
Low Collective Efficacy	*Low Collective Efficacy*
Low Teacher Credibility	*High Teacher Credibility*

"THE AMPLIFIER": HIGH COLLECTIVE EFFICACY/HIGH TEACHER CREDIBILITY

Jamillah Newton is a valued member of her high school science department. She has a well-deserved reputation among current and former students as being highly credible. She is quiet and unassuming in most circumstances, but she comes alive in her classroom. Although her biology class is known to be academically demanding, her students consistently achieve, sometimes surprising themselves with their accomplishments. A National Board Certified Teacher, Ms. Newton strives to deepen her practice each year. As such, she actively seeks feedback from her team, especially junior colleagues. "Their questions cause me to think about ideas I take for granted," she says. Ms. Newton encourages people to visit, and often volunteers to be the first to try new approaches on behalf of the team. When the school began to utilize microteaching for professional learning, Ms. Newton immediately asked if she could use it. She video recorded a portion of a lesson, reviewed it herself, then shared the clip with her team to ask questions about how she might improve. Ms. Newton understands that her reputation as an excellent teacher might be perceived as intimidating; therefore she is deliberate in being vulnerable. Little wonder that she is regularly sought out to advise on many work committees at the school and district.

NOTES

Why are amplifiers such valuable team members? Describe the characteristics of an amplifier you've worked with.

"THE INDEPENDENT CONTRACTOR": LOW COLLECTIVE EFFICACY/HIGH TEACHER CREDIBILITY

Middle school English teacher Antoinette Richardson is widely known in her school as a credible teacher. Her students often quote Ms. Richardson in discussions, and they report that the writing instruction she delivers in her English classroom is intense, but worth it. Her colleagues agree—they have seen the effects of Ms. Richardson's instruction as students write in their own subjects. But she is something of an enigma to the adults in the school. It's not that she isn't pleasant or sociable; she is. But she rarely contributes to the team, usually just nodding in silent agreement. However, she doesn't put many of their ideas into play in her classroom. While she has received several teaching awards, she holds herself at a distance from other adults. "I know what I'm doing, so I really don't need input from others," she says. Ms. Richardson doesn't invite others into her classroom and infrequently shares successes or challenges she is facing. "I do my job, and I do it well," says Ms. Richardson. "If I wanted to spend my time teaching teachers, I'd be an administrator."

When an "independent contractor" is a member, there is a loss to the team.

iStock.com/track5

PAUSE & PONDER

What is lost to the team when an independent contractor is a member? In what ways is the independent contractor's professional growth limited?

"THE TALKER": HIGH COLLECTIVE EFFICACY/ LOW TEACHER CREDIBILITY

Everyone enjoys Millicent Anderson's company at their third-grade team meetings. She is brimming with ideas, reads professional journals, and enjoys talking about teaching. In spite of that, she doesn't appear to put much of what she learns into action in her own classroom. Her chief classroom management strategy seems to be authoritarian; students spend large periods of time in independent reading or writing, and are reminded to do so silently. She has an elaborate daily calendar routine that lasts 45 minutes and doesn't vary. Her room is filled with the trappings of learning, with lots of books and designated areas for activities. She claims that she uses an inquiry approach to learning, but it lacks an appropriate level of rigor. Direct instruction seldom occurs, as has been witnessed by her colleagues. She invites others into her classroom, but there's not much to see, as little changes across the school year. The principal strategically assigns students to Ms. Anderson's class who are quiet and compliant. Her colleagues like her, but they wonder why they are working so hard when it doesn't seem like Millicent does.

It's easy to overlook a talker's shortcomings, because talkers are personable.

iStock.com/SDI Productions

PAUSE & PONDER

It's easy to overlook a talker's shortcomings, because talkers are personable. How might the learning of the talker's students be at risk?

"THE LONER": LOW COLLECTIVE EFFICACY/LOW TEACHER CREDIBILITY

Kyle Henderson's ninth-grade algebra classes are to be endured, say his students. They are regular visitors to their high school's guidance office as they seek to transfer to another mathematics teacher. Mr. Henderson doesn't think much of them, either. He is harsh and short with them, confining most of his communication to algebra. His colleagues routinely field student complaints about Mr. Henderson, and while they try to remain as neutral as possible, they are at a loss for how to respond. To be clear, Mr. Henderson is a pleasant colleague, but his colleagues confine their interactions to nonschool conversations. His fellow math teachers increasingly avoid his classroom, as they know that it's likely they will have to help him manage the consistently disrespectful exchanges between him and his students. At professional learning community meetings, Kyle usually has his arms folded defensively and rarely contributes beyond listing this week's problems. Privately, he fumes about the administration, believing that if they had a harsher discipline code, everything would be fine. He attributes his colleagues' success to the luck of the draw: "They got the good kids." He is beginning to believe the advice his college roommate gave him. Teaching just isn't worth it. Maybe he should give his friend a call about that marketing job he's been bragging about.

The loner is at risk personally and professionally. So are the loner's students.
iStock.com/DGLimages

The loner is at risk personally and professionally. So are the loner's students. What experiences have you had with supporting a loner?

CONCLUDING THOUGHTS ABOUT TEACHER CREDIBILITY AND COLLECTIVE EFFICACY

Maybe we haven't been transparent enough. We want you to be successful with students, and we want you to love your job. And we think that one of the best ways to have success is to develop your credibility. As we think you'll see, credibility has the power to transform your career and ensure that students learn a lot. In terms of loving your job, it's easier to love work when you have productive relationships with your coworkers. Teaching is a complex and demanding job. We don't have to go it alone. We're better with our colleagues, especially when we don't have to reinvent the proverbial wheel. In addition, you'll like your job better when you see the impact that you have on students. It's really not about how hard you work; it's about the results. And when the results are in, all that work will be worth it.

Nancy provides you with a challenge to conclude this chapter, as she will do in each chapter. In essence, she asks that you think about the type of teacher you are and who you want to be. Consider the ways in which teacher credibility and collective efficacy could impact your professional life.

IT'S EASIER TO LOVE WORK WHEN YOU HAVE PRODUCTIVE RELATIONSHIPS WITH YOUR COWORKERS.

CHAPTER 1 CHALLENGE

What type of teacher are you and who do you want to be?

TRUST

noun | trust | \ ˈtrəst \

a: Assured reliance on the character, ability, strength, or truth of someone or something

b: One in which confidence is placed

CHAPTER 2
FOCUSES ON
trust as perceived
by students. Trust is
an important part of
teacher credibility
and impacts teams
of adults as they
collaborate.

CREATING AND MAINTAINING TRUST WITH STUDENTS

The first dimension of teacher credibility is **trust**. Students want to know that their teachers are trustworthy. When he was in elementary school, Dominique's son had a teacher who violated the trust of students on a fairly regular basis. As you read that sentence, you might think of some terrible action that an adult took. But breeching trust can be much more subtle than that. This particular teacher did several things that compromised her students' belief that she was trustworthy. She was a generally pleasant person who seemed like she could teach well. But the boy's educational experience was compromised as a result of the lack of trust.

First, the teacher would regularly make promises but then not keep them. For example, she said that if the class got to 100 points for their collective behavior, they would have a party. When the time came and they had earned the points, she delayed, even though students would ask about the party on a regular basis. In fact, the promised party never came. We could spend time on the problematic approach to classroom management in which everyone had to act a certain way for the class to get points, which caused all kinds of stress and tension in the class, not to mention the targeting of some students because of their behavior. But the fact that she made a promise and failed to deliver on it undermined the trust that the students had in her. There may have been very good reasons that she could not have the party, but she never explained the reasons to the class.

If this were the only broken promise, it's possible there wouldn't have been too much damage. But there were other incidents that chipped away at the perception that she was reliable. She told the class about fieldtrips, some of which did not happen. She made simple promises to do things, such as finishing a chapter of a favorite book in the afternoon, but then forgot or got busy.

She also violated trust as part of her classroom management. She sent a letter home to families explaining that students who did not have a good week would have a "Bummer Friday," which required that they do additional seat work while classmates watched movies as a reward. Again, we could comment about the problems with this approach, including the use of instructional minutes to watch movies unrelated to the content. The real problem was that she focused her attention on catching students doing things wrong and then commenting on it publicly.

As Dominique's son said, "There are some bad kids in our class, and they always have Bummer Friday. But I'm scared that I'm going to get it, because she's always trying to catch you." Sadly, Dominique's son thought that there were "bad kids" in his class, because the

Introducing Trust.

LISTEN as Doug introduces the value of trust in schools.

classroom management system did not provide them with alternatives to learn prosocial behaviors.

The third way she violated trust centered on her feedback to students about their performance. She routinely assigned homework but did not review it. Again, we could comment on the appropriateness of the homework she gave, but trust would suggest that she would review the tasks she assigned rather than collecting it and then allowing students to see their work in the recycle bin. As part of her feedback, she praised students for their work, even when the quality was low. One memorable time, Dominique's son had football practice and fell asleep in the car on the way home. Thus, he did not finish his writing assignment. In the morning, he did what he could, but his work was clearly not up to his regular standard. In spite of this, during the writing conference later that day, the teacher praised his work and did not comment on the errors or length. Dominique's son talked about it that night, saying, "She said I did a good job, but I really didn't."

Again, this was a well-meaning teacher. She did not scream at students. Her lessons were generally strong, and she used appropriate instructional strategies. It's just that her students didn't trust her, and thus their learning was diminished as a result. We believe that she was doing what she thought was best. But she didn't realize the power of teacher credibility. In other words, she had not learned the lesson that Covey (2008) tried to teach us in *The Speed of Trust*: when trust exists, things go faster. That applies to learning as well.

Students want to know that their teachers are trustworthy.
iStock.com/SDI Productions

A simple definition of trust involves truth and reliability of information. But when it comes to complex organizations like schools, the definition of trust is more complex. We have adopted the definition of trust proposed by Hoy and Tschannen-Moran (2003): "Trust is an individual's or group's willingness to be vulnerable to another party based on the confidence that the latter party is benevolent, reliable, competent, honest, and open" (p. 189). We appreciate this definition, because it acknowledges that we must be vulnerable if we are to develop trust. And that goes for students as well as our professional peers. But for now, we will focus on trust between students and teachers.

> "WE INHABIT A CLIMATE OF TRUST AS WE INHABIT AN ATMOSPHERE AND NOTICE IT AS WE NOTICE AIR, ONLY WHEN IT BECOMES SCARCE OR POLLUTED" (BAIER, 1994, P. 98).

Annette Baier, a New Zealand philosopher, made an interesting observation about trust when she wrote, "We inhabit a climate of trust as we inhabit an atmosphere and notice it as we notice air, only when it becomes scarce or polluted" (1994, p. 98). That is what happened to Dominique's son. Trust became obvious when it was scarce. As educators, we need to ensure that trust is not scarce or polluted, because this damages our credibility and thus student learning. Trust should be in the air, all around students, so that they can learn. To accomplish this, we need to attend to the five elements named in Hoy and Tschannen-Moran's definition, including (as defined by von Frank, 2010):

- **Benevolence:** Confidence that one's well-being or something one cares about will be protected by the trusted party . . . the assurance that others will not exploit one's vulnerability or take advantage even when the opportunity is available.

- **Honesty:** The trusted person's character, integrity, and authenticity . . . acceptance of responsibility for one's actions and not distorting the truth in order to shift blame to another.

- **Openness:** The extent to which relevant information is shared . . . openness signals reciprocal trust.

- **Reliability:** Consistency of behavior and knowing what to expect from others . . . a sense of confidence that one's needs will be met in positive ways.

- **Competency:** The ability to perform as expected and according to standards appropriate to the task at hand. (p. 2)

REFLECTIVE WRITING

How did the five dimensions of trust presented by Hoy and Tschannen-Moran (2003) compare with your original thinking about trust?

Consider the five elements of trust. Using the "traffic light" scale, identify your trustworthiness across these five dimensions.

- This is an area of concern. I need to pause and figure out how to improve.
- This is an area of uncertainty. I will proceed with caution knowing there is room for improvement.
- This is an area of strength.

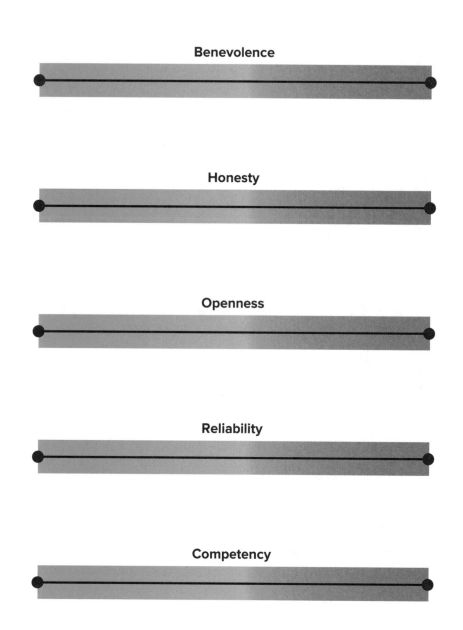

Benevolence

Honesty

Openness

Reliability

Competency

PAUSE & PONDER

What do you see as your strengths, and what areas need attention?

A MEASUREMENT OF TRUST

If you want to get a sense of the level of trust in your classroom or school, you can use the *Student Trust in Faculty Scale* (Adams & Forsyth, 2009). This tool is based on the five aspects of trust identified above, and yet it is very brief (10 items), which makes it useful for student administrations (see Figure 2.1). The researchers developed the tool to "capture student perceptions and recollections of teacher behavior, which allow for judgments to be made about their relative openness, benevolence, reliability, competence, and honesty" (p. 264). It is important to administer this assessment confidentially so that trust is maintained. Participants should be told that their participation is voluntary and that they will suffer no penalty for refusing to complete the survey. They should also be told that they may skip any items they are uncomfortable answering. The scoring directions from the authors include the following:

- Step 1: Calculate the average score for each survey participant by taking the mean of all 10 items of the Student Trust in Faculty scale.

- Step 2: Calculate the grand mean score on the Student Trust in Faculty scale for your school by taking an average of all of the participants' individual scores.

- Step 3: Compute the Standardized Score for Student Trust in Faculty. In this step you will convert your school's grand mean score to a standardized score with a mean of 500 and a standard deviation of 100, making comparison with other schools possible.

    1. First compute the difference between your school's grand mean score on student trust in faculty (STF) and the mean for the normative sample. For a high school, this would mean (STF − 3.059).

    2. Next, multiply the difference by one hundred [100(STF − 3.059)].

    3. Divide the product by the standard deviation of the normative sample (.728).

    4. Add 500 to the result. You now have computed a standardized score: your Standardized Score for Student Trust in Faculty.

For middle or elementary schools, use the appropriate formula below. Remember that the student trust survey has a five-point response scale. For high schools, calculate your standardized score using the following formula:

Standardized Score for Student Trust in Faculty (STF) = 100(STF − 3.059)/.728 + 500 (as described above)

For middle schools, calculate your standardized trust score using the following formula:

Standardized Score for Student Trust in Faculty (STF) =
100(STF − 3.142)/.861 + 500

For elementary schools, calculate your standardized trust score using the following formula:

Standardized Score for Student Trust in Faculty (STF) =
100(STF − 4.107)/.781 + 500

NOTES

Figure 2.1 Student Trust in Faculty Scale

Student Survey — *Directions:* Please tell us how much you agree or disagree with each of the statements about your school by filling in the bubbles on the right, choosing from (1) Strongly Disagree, (2) Disagree, (3) Neither Agree nor Disagree, (4) Agree, or (5) Strongly Agree.	Strongly Disagree	Disagree	Neither Agree nor Disagree	Agree	Strongly Agree
1. Teachers are always ready to help.	①	②	③	④	⑤
2. Teachers are easy to talk to at this school.	①	②	③	④	⑤
3. Students learn a lot from teachers in this school.	①	②	③	④	⑤
4. Students at this school can depend on teachers for help.	①	②	③	④	⑤
5. Teachers at this school do a terrific job.	①	②	③	④	⑤
6. Teachers at this school really listen to students.	①	②	③	④	⑤
7. Teachers always do what they are supposed to do.	①	②	③	④	⑤
8. Students are well cared for at this school.	①	②	③	④	⑤
9. Teachers at this school are good at teaching.	①	②	③	④	⑤
10. Teachers at this school are always honest with me.	①	②	③	④	⑤

Source: Adams, C.M., & Forsyth, P.B. (2009). Conceptualizing and validating a measure of student trust. In: Hoy, W.K. and DiPaola, M., Eds., *Studies in School Improvement*, 47, 263–279. Charlotte, NC: Information Age Publishing.

The tool uses a mean of 500 and a standard deviation of 100, which allows you to create a standardized score and compare the scores of your classroom or school with those from a national sample. As noted by the authors, the range of the standardized scores is as follows:

- If the score is 200, it is lower than 99% of the schools.
- If the score is 300, it is lower than 97% of the schools.
- If the score is 400, it is lower than 84% of the schools.
- If the score is 500, it is average.
- If the score is 600, it is higher than 84% of the schools.
- If the score is 700, it is higher than 97% of the schools.
- If the score is 800, it is higher than 99% of the schools.

Data are powerful but need to be used wisely. Hoy and Tschannen-Moran note that focusing on trust is much like studying the roots of a plant. Without care, the examination can damage or destroy the very thing you are trying to learn about.

REFLECTIVE WRITING

What could the data from the student trust survey teach you?

Before you collect these data, ask yourself these questions:

- What is our purpose for gathering these data?
- What is the scope of the data collection?
- Who will gather the data? By when?

_____

_____

_____

_____

_____

_____

_____

_____

_____

Once you have the data collected, ask yourself these questions:

- What did I learn about trust in my classroom or school?
- How can I increase my trustworthiness with students?
- What can I learn from my colleagues about trustworthiness?

_____

_____

_____

_____

_____

_____

_____

_____

_____

_____

_____

_____

_____

_____

USE TRUST DATA TO TAKE ACTION

The teachers at Cypress Springs Middle School understood the caution and yet knew that they needed to address the issue of trust in their school. Their survey results suggested that they were lower than 84% of schools, and they theorized that was why their students' academic achievement was so low. But even more than that, the teachers regularly commented about students' apathy for learning and their lack of engagement in lessons.

When they analyzed their data, the teachers noted that the lowest average was for the question about listening. Math teacher Paul Hart commented, "The question is whether or not we really listen to students. Their answer is a resounding no, at least on this survey. I'm interested in why students might say that."

Lynn Duffy, the inclusion support teacher on the team, responded. "I think it's a time in their life when they want more control and want to be heard. But maybe we haven't provided a forum for them to tell us what they want us to know."

"I'm concerned about this," added Anthony Nesmith, an English teacher, "I want students to be heard. I think we all need to learn more about active listening. I think we need a schoolwide campaign on listening and then time in our department meetings to talk about what we hear from students."

"I agree," Mr. Hart continued. "I think that this would be a great focus. But I'd like to comment on a few other items. First, the students do think that they are cared for, which is great. They also think we do a terrific job, which is nice to hear. But the second lowest area, after listening, is that we're not very easy to talk to. I think we need to make ourselves more accessible as part of our focus on listening. I'm going to make a point of standing in the hallway during passing periods to talk with students. I used to do that a lot, but I've gotten lazy and just greet students when they come into the classroom. So, I really only talk with my current students. I hardly ever see former students. I think being present in the hallway can help this."

Ms. Duffy picked up the conversation, adding, "I agree. And I'll make that commitment as well. I also think we need to revisit the class meetings and circles that we used to do. I remember having a class meeting each week, with an agenda and everything. Students ran the meeting and had a voice in my class."

A sample class meeting agenda can be found in Figure 2.2.

Figure 2.2 Sample class meeting schedule

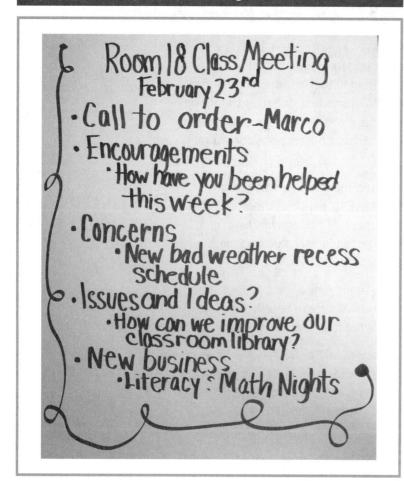

Room 18 Class Meeting
February 23rd
• Call to order—Marco
• Encouragements
    • How have you been helped this week?
• Concerns
    • New bad weather recess schedule
• Issues and Ideas?
    • How can we improve our classroom library?
• New business
    • Literacy & Math Nights

The meeting is typically chaired by a student. There are many variations on class meetings, but they typically include peer recognition and some ability to address concerns.

Mr. Nesmith responded, "I think that there is work to be done in this area. I'll accept the challenge of spending passing periods in the hallways. And I think that I'll focus on circles, too. I think I've neglected that and want to bring it back so that students learn to listen to each other and that I take time to listen to them."

There are generally two types of circles or reasons to have circles:

- *Informal classroom circles* to discuss content and issues that impact the group.

- *Formal classroom circles* to resolve a problem that resides within the group.

But the structure of the circles can vary. Regardless of the type, students are literally seated in a circle, ideally with nothing in front of them (no desk or table). There is a symbolic talking item that can be used in some circles. We commonly see the following options, all of which work for informal and formal circles:

○ **Sequential**—Students speak in order, with the conversation traveling around the circle in order. Depending on the topic, students can pass if they want.

○ **Nonsequential**—Students speak as they want, with the current speaker recognizing the next speaker.

○ **Fishbowl**—A smaller group of students sits in a circle inside a larger circle that contains the rest of the class. An empty chair or two is available in the inside circle so that members from the outer circle can join when they have something to add.

○ **Inside-Outside**—The students are divided into two groups. One group forms an inside circle facing outward. Members of the other group form an outside circle facing the student that they will be speaking with. After a predetermined amount of time, students in the outer circle rotate clockwise.

Mr. Nesmith restarted his circles with sequential circles that were informal in nature. The topics ranged from expectations for the week to the stress students were experiencing based on an upcoming test.

THINK ALONG

Circle Meeting. Listen as Dominique shares his thinking. As you do, consider the following questions:

- What experiences have you had with circles or class meetings?
- What are the potential benefits of this practice?
- What advice do you have for others or yourself?

They were ready for the conversation when they needed a formal circle to discuss some bullying comments that were posted on social media. As one of the students commented after the circle, "I feel a lot better. I wasn't sure what to do when I saw the posts, and now I know what I want to do. I feel that we all listened to each other, and Mr. Nesmith listened to us without judging us."

REFLECTIVE WRITING

As you think about Mr. Nesmith's story, consider the following reflective questions:

- Do I deliver what I say I am going to deliver?
- Do I act in such a way that I would trust me?
- Do I personify the five aspects of trust: benevolence, honesty, openness, reliability, competency?

REGAIN TRUST WHEN IT HAS BEEN DAMAGED

Trust is easier to gain than regain. Thus far, we have focused on creating and maintaining trust. But sometimes trust is violated or broken and needs to be rebuilt.

REFLECTIVE WRITING

What have been your experiences with regaining trust with colleagues when it has been damaged? Which of the recommendations from this chapter might help?

We will turn our attention to teacher-student relationships later in this chapter, but for now, some of the ways that trust can be rebuilt include the following:

- **Apologize**. When you make a mistake, own it and apologize. Yes, especially to students. We are all human and we all make mistakes. An apology can go a long way toward rebuilding trust.

- **Listen**. When trust has been broken, it is time to listen more intently. You have to learn where the hurt lies so that you can address that hurt. Recovery begins with acknowledgment. Sometimes, students need time to vent. If you broke trust with students, they will need some time to vent to move past the hurt. Of course, you are still the adult, and there are parameters about student conduct. You may want to invite a colleague to mediate the conversation.

ONCE TRUST IS VIOLATED, IT IS HUMAN NATURE TO LOOK FOR ADDITIONAL EVIDENCE THAT THE PERSON IS NOT TRUSTWORTHY.

- **Make amends but not promises you cannot keep**. Your goal is to make things right, but in doing so, don't make the problem worse by making a promise you can't keep. Amends can come in a range of ways, from direct approaches such as fixing physical damage to indirect approaches such as providing time.

- **Allow time**. As the saying goes, "time heals all wounds." Sometimes, depending on the damage done, you might need a light touch with a student or group of students. Don't shy away from them, but recognize that it may take some time for them to trust you again.

- **Be reliable**. Once trust is violated, it is human nature to look for additional evidence that the person is not trustworthy. Redouble your efforts to be reliable. Follow through on your promises.

- **Forgive yourself**. As we noted before, we are human and, as such, fallible. But sometimes we forget to forgive ourselves. That is not to say that we ignore the consequences of our actions, but rather that we come to terms with them and learn to forgive.

USE TRUST TO BUILD TEACHER-STUDENT RELATIONSHIPS

To paraphrase educator Rita Pierson, young people don't learn from old people they don't like. In addition to our collective personal knowledge about the power of humane, growth-producing relationships, there is compelling research evidence to support this. We have already noted that teacher credibility has an effect size of 1.09, which is impressive. And we have noted that credibility has four components. But if we just consider teacher-student relationships, the effect size is .48, still above average and likely to further accelerate learning. There is a distinction between teacher credibility and teacher-student relationships. The former operates in one direction and lies within the student's perceptions. The latter is bidirectional, as both teacher and student participate in its development. These are not unrelated to one another, and in fact trust is foundational in relationships. As Marzano (2011) notes,

> *Positive relationships between teachers and students are among the most commonly cited variables associated with effective instruction. If the relationship is strong, instructional strategies seem to be more effective. Conversely, a weak or negative relationship will mute or even negate the benefits of even the most effective instructional strategies.* (p. 82)

YOUNG PEOPLE DON'T LEARN FROM OLD PEOPLE THEY DON'T LIKE.

The Search Institute has created a Developmental Relationships Framework (see Figure 2.3). Their model has five major components (expressed from the perspective of an individual student), including the following:

- Express care—show me that I matter to you.
- Challenge growth—push me to keep getting better.
- Provide support—help me complete tasks and achieve goals.
- Share power—treat me with respect and give me a say.
- Expand possibilities—connect me with people and places that broaden my world.

Figure 2.3 The Developmental Relationships Framework

The Developmental Relationships Framework

Young people are more likely to grow up successfully when they experience developmental relationships with important people in their lives. Developmental relationships are close connections through which young people discover who they are, cultivate abilities to shape their own lives, and learn how to engage with and contribute to the world around them. Search Institute has identified five elements—expressed in 20 specific actions—that make relationships powerful in young people's lives.

Elements	Actions	Definitions
Express Care Show me that I matter to you.	• **Be dependable**	Be someone I can trust.
	• **Listen**	Really pay attention when we are together.
	• **Believe in me**	Make me feel known and valued.
	• **Be warm**	Show me you enjoy being with me.
	• **Encourage**	Praise me for my efforts and achievements.
Challenge Growth Push me to keep getting better.	• **Expect my best**	Expect me to live up to my potential.
	• **Stretch**	Push me to go further.
	• **Hold me accountable**	Insist I take responsibility for my actions.
	• **Reflect on failures**	Help me learn from mistakes and setbacks.
Provide Support Help me complete tasks and achieve goals.	• **Navigate**	Guide me through hard situations and systems.
	• **Empower**	Build my confidence to take charge of my life.
	• **Advocate**	Stand up for me when I need it.
	• **Set boundaries**	Put limits in place that keep me on track.
Share Power Treat me with respect and give me a say.	• **Respect me**	Take me seriously and treat me fairly.
	• **Include me**	Involve me in decisions that affect me.
	• **Collaborate**	Work with me to solve problems and reach goals.
	• **Let me lead**	Create opportunities for me to take action and lead.
Expand Possibilities Connect me with people and places that broaden my world.	• **Inspire**	Inspire me to see possibilities for my future.
	• **Broaden horizons**	Expose me to new ideas, experiences, and places.
	• **Connect**	Introduce me to people who can help me grow.

Note: Relationships are, by definition, bidirectional, with each person giving and receiving. So each person in a strong relationship both engages in and experiences each of these actions. However, for the purpose of clarity, this framework is expressed from the perspective of one young person.

Note that each of the major components has actions and definitions. For example, one of the actions is to advocate. *Stand up for me when I need it.* This is one of 20 actions, all of which are powerful. As an example of advocacy, a teacher we know was concerned about a specific student's discipline based on an accusation of plagiarism in her dual-enrollment college class. The student was told that she had failed the assignment, that she would need to take a timed essay test, and that her grade on the timed test would be averaged with the zero for the essay that she submitted. Importantly, the professor used a commercially available plagiarism checking program, which did not identify any lines that had been taken from another source. The high school teacher contacted the community college faculty member to advocate for the student, saying "The software didn't identify any plagiarism. I was her 11th-grade English teacher, and she really is a top student. Where do you think she plagiarized?" The college faculty member's response demonstrated her lack of trust for students when she said, "I just think the writing is above the level of a high school student. It's better than that of most of my college students."

The high school teacher reminded the community college faculty member that this particular student was not planning to attend a community college in the fall, but rather had been accepted into a well-known university, adding, "Yes, she is a high school student and a very talented one. Perhaps you're not used to the level of writing of students who immediately enroll in four-year universities. I'm worried about ruining her GPA, but more important, I'm concerned that teachers should make claims of impropriety based on evidence. Before contacting you, I Googled several lines of her essay and ran a separate analysis with our software program, and I can't find any evidence that these aren't her words. I would be happy to share with you some of her essays from last year if you want to see the quality of her writing."

Unfortunately, the college faculty member was not persuaded to accept the essay, but she did agree that if the student's performance on the timed exam demonstrated a similar level of skill, the score would stand and would not be averaged with a zero. The student did do very well on the timed essay, and her grade was not negatively impacted.

When Dominique asked her about the situation, she told him, "I guess that I'm going to always encounter people who don't believe in me. It's a life lesson. But I also learned that there are people who have your back—who do something that they don't have to do because they care. I have mad respect for the teachers here. They protect us and challenge us, and we're better because of it."

Consider each of the factors from the Developmental Relationships Framework. Use the scale on the left to estimate the number of students who believe that you demonstrate each factor.

Express care—

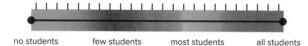

no students　few students　most students　all students

show me that I matter to you.

Challenge growth—

no students　few students　most students　all students

push me to keep getting better.

Provide support—

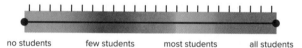

no students　few students　most students　all students

help me complete tasks and achieve goals.

Share power—

no students　few students　most students　all students

treat me with respect and give me a say.

Expand possibilities—

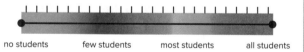

no students　few students　most students　all students

connect me with people and places that broaden my world.

Take a look at your responses. What do you notice? What are your strengths and opportunities for growth? Are you willing to share your responses with a trusted peer and solicit advice?

THINK ALONG

Building Relationships.
Listen as Dominique talks about ways to build relationships. How might you use this information to strengthen the relationships you have with students?

The Search Institute's Developmental Relationships Framework contains useful information about actions that educators can take to ensure that relationships are powerful. As they noted (see Figure 2.3), "Relationships are, by definition, bidirectional, with each person giving and receiving. So, each person in a strong relationship both engages in and experiences each of these actions." In other words, it's not just teachers who do those things for students, but also students who engage in these same actions for their peers and their teachers. Some of the ways that we have seen teachers develop healthy, growth-producing relationships with students include these:

- **Knowing their names and how to pronounce them**. This may seem obvious, but students often report that their teachers don't know their names. In fact, in the national MyVoice survey by Russ Quaglia, 52% of students in grades 3–12 indicated that they didn't believe their teachers knew their names (Quaglia & Corso, 2014). Make a commitment to learn all of your students' names. Make sure you pronounce their names correctly as well.

- **Say hello and good-bye to every student every day.** There are any number of ways to do this. Looking at each student and greeting her or him conveys that the student is valuable and worth your time. Some teachers invite students to choose their greetings, such as a handshake, high-five, or hug (if allowed in the district). Others stand at the door and greet each student as the student enters the room. We find that more teachers say hello individually than good-bye. But one teacher we know stands at the door at the end of each period and high-fives students on the way out, saying each student's name and making a comment about their accomplishments for the day. As one of her students said, "I'm excited for the end of class, not because it's over but because I get to hear what my teacher has to say about my effort that day."

- **Know their interests and attend extracurricular events.** Students will play harder, dance better, and sing louder when you are in the audience. You are a superhero, and they are thrilled when you are present at their events. We have lost count of the number of times a student finished a game or performance and ran up to a teacher, asking the teacher to meet his or her parents. We also notice that students whose parents aren't able to attend stand proudly next to their teachers. Remember to attend events that are outside of your personal interests. Dominique is a big sports fan, but you can also find him visiting the chess club, the anime group, and every play and poetry slam that students are part of.

- **Speak with respect.** Again, this may seem obvious, but we have also lost count of the number of times we have heard harsh or sarcastic words come from a teacher. It damages relationships and prevents students from bonding with the adult who is there to teach them. Your words are powerful.

- **Monitor nonverbal communication.** Estimates are that more than half of our communication is nonverbal.

It's not just the words we use with students; it is also our body language. And students are always paying attention to the messages we send. Eye rolls, crossed arms, and defensive stances send powerful negative messages to

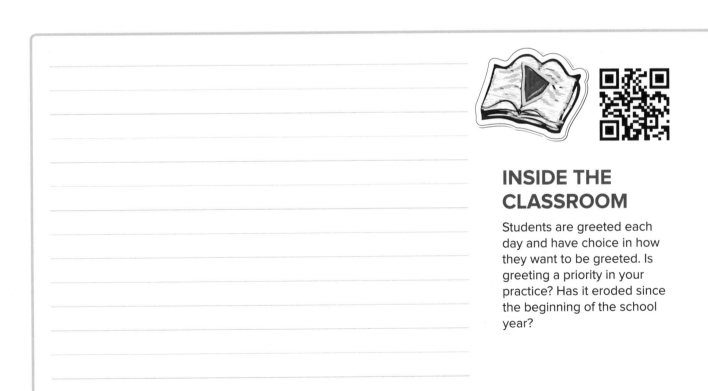

INSIDE THE CLASSROOM

Students are greeted each day and have choice in how they want to be greeted. Is greeting a priority in your practice? Has it eroded since the beginning of the school year?

REFLECTIVE WRITING

Identify a hard-to-reach student. How would you describe the current condition of your relationship with him or her? What are current growth opportunities in the five dimensions?

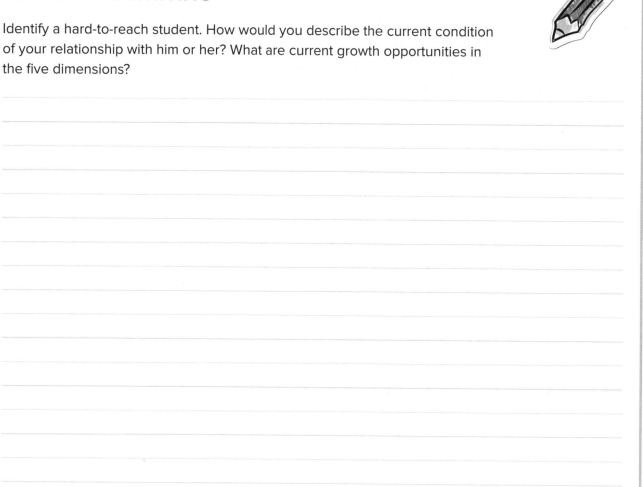

students about the approachability of an adult and whether or not this adult is one to trust and value.

- **Share your world**. No, not necessarily your entire personal life, but your world. Young students are surprised to learn that you buy groceries and sometimes even eat out, just like them. They want to know more about you, and you should share aspects of your life appropriate for school. Dominique tells students stories about his three children and their antics. Nancy talks about visiting family members who live in other states. Doug entertains students by talking about movies and books he likes and dislikes. Your everyday lives give them insight into your humanity.

We made that seem really easy. And actually, it is. It's a choice. We can focus our energy on developing relationships with students because we know it matters. Or, we can ignore the evidence of the social and emotional dimensions of learning at our own peril. These same principles of trust apply to the working relationships we have with our colleagues.

COLLECTIVE EFFICACY AND TRUST

Trust in the organization is crucial in order for schools to operate at high levels (Hoy & Tschannen-Moran, 2003). Trust in the organization operates in two directions for teachers:

1. Trust in the principal
2. Trust in colleagues

Similar to students' trust in their teachers, teachers' trust in the principal means that teachers perceive that the school leader keeps promises, is truthful, and holds the best interests of teachers in mind when making decisions (Tschannen-Moran & Hoy, 1998). Trust in our colleagues means that we can count on them in challenging situations. Tschannen-Moran and Hoy and other researchers assert that collegial trust is even more important than trust in the principal, perhaps because colleagues have more frequent interactions with one another than with the principal. In a large part, this is because trust is foundational to collective efficacy.

The four dimensions of collective efficacy are as follows (Bandura, 1993):

1. **Experiences of Mastery**. The experience of mastery is the single most important factor developing and reinforcing efficacy. When we experience success or accomplishments, we begin to attribute those successes to our actions rather than outside forces. In other words, success breeds success. We look for situations in which we believe we will be successful, because they reinforce our self-efficacy. Conversely, we tend to avoid situations in which we believe we will fail. Or, if we already have limited efficacy, we look for confirming evidence that we are not going to be successful.

2. **Modeling**. When we see others succeed, especially when we perceive them to be about the same as ourselves, our self-efficacy increases. To a large extent, people say to themselves, "If they can do it, so can I." Modeling experiences provide us with examples of what is possible. Importantly, these models need to result in positive outcomes if we are to be encouraged to try that which was modeled for us.

3. **Social Persuasion**. To a lesser extent, encouragement from others builds self-efficacy. We say *to a lesser extent,* because the previous two factors are very powerful. But we don't want to ignore the power of peer support.

WHEN WE EXPERIENCE SUCCESS OR ACCOMPLISHMENTS, WE BEGIN TO ATTRIBUTE THOSE SUCCESSES TO OUR ACTIONS RATHER THAN OUTSIDE FORCES.

When we trust the person who encourages us, we can increase our self-efficacy. If the person is honest with us, and we believe that that person has our best interests at heart, social persuasion can serve as a tipping point.

4. **Physiological Factors**. There are a number of physical and biological contributors to our self-efficacy. When we experience stress, our self-efficacy is generally reduced—that is, unless we learn to recognize that stress as part of a natural process. Similarly, when we are frightened, it's hard to maintain self-efficacy. Instead, we move into a flight, fight, or freeze situation. People with higher levels of self-efficacy recognize these physiological factors and understand that they are natural biological responses to situations that do not necessarily signal failure.

The first two speak to our own experiences and those of others, while the last two—social persuasion and physiological factors—address the relational aspects of collective efficacy.

REFLECTIVE WRITING

How can the four dimensions of collective efficacy be used to build trust?

It is here that trust contributes to a team's confidence, so that they can positively impact student learning. Social persuasion refers to the ways we make decisions about the reliability of information. In other words, we consider the source, not just the message, to make judgments about whether we will accept or reject the information. Our affective state, which comprises the psychological and physiological responses we have when we communicate, further influences our receptivity to the message. Trust underpins both phenomena.

The daily work we do with colleagues is continually recalibrated through a lens of trustworthiness. As noted previously, trust is not consciously noticed until it has been violated. A colleague who does not follow through with decisions made by the team reduces her own trustworthiness. If this occurs repeatedly, the team may feel it is less able to effect change.

That's what happened when a fourth-grade team made plans to repurpose a grade-level writing rubric they had created to foster more self-assessment habits with their students. One member of the team had proven herself to be unreliable in implementing grade-wide instructional practices, and she did not have much credibility with her students, who openly complained about being placed with her. After all, the children would hear what their friends were doing in their classes, only to discover they would not be doing so in their own. This was an open secret among the other teachers. You could see teachers tense up when this teacher spoke, and they sometimes doubted the veracity of what she had to say. That said, the team never directly addressed the tension present in the room at every meeting. However, the real damage occurred when a new fourth-grade teacher arrived at the school. Having observed that there seemed to be little internal accountability within the team, she too began to disregard decisions she didn't like. What had begun as a small crack in trust had splintered the team, and the overall effect was a concurrent reduction in their collective efficacy.

Without accountability to ourselves as a collective, we damage the normative expectations we hold for ourselves and our students. When collegial trust is compromised, one's social persuasion is reduced. We "consider the source" and disregard the information, even when it might otherwise be valuable. Over time, this becomes the proverbial baggage that teams drag with them. But it is rare for teams to be given the tools to regain trust when it has been violated. School leaders can play an important role in assisting a team that has suffered from simmering trust issues by holding private meetings with the person who has been unreliable. The goal of these meetings is to conduct a humane and growth-producing discussion with the team, facilitated by the school leader. While these can be hard conversations to hold, they are necessary if the collective efficacy of the school is to be upheld.

In preparation for later chapters in this book, capture the essence of each factor that builds collective efficacy in 10 words or fewer. Keep these factors in mind as you read this book and as you interact with your colleagues.

EXPERIENCES OF MASTERY	MODELING

SOCIAL PERSUASION	PHYSIOLOGICAL FACTORS

What have you noticed about the collective efficacy of your team? What experiences have you had that have contributed to the collective efficacy of your team? What experiences have lowered it?

EXPERIENCES THAT BUILD MY SELF-EFFICACY	EXPERIENCES THAT LOWER MY SELF-EFFICACY
•	•
•	•
•	•

TRUST

CONCLUDING THOUGHTS ABOUT TRUST

Simply said, trust matters for students and colleagues, and it is foundational to the relationships we establish. As we have noted, these relationships are a grist for learning. They make it safe for students to take risks and chance being wrong. And they help students develop into productive members of their communities. Yet, they are only part of what makes a teacher credible. Importantly, all of the other teachers at a school know which teachers have productive relationships with students and which do not. And this takes a different toll, specifically on the collective efficacy of the team. We will eventually focus our attention more fully on collective efficacy. Relationships and trust are worth the investment and pay dividends for years, especially when a student returns and asks, *Do you remember me?*

Nancy provides you with a challenge to conclude this chapter. In essence, she asks,

Do you trust yourself? Are you a trustworthy person? She then offers you a challenge to grow in the area of trust.

CHAPTER 2 CHALLENGE

Do you trust yourself? Are you a trustworthy person?

COMPETENCE

noun | com·pe·tence | \ ˈkäm-pə-tən(t)s \

The quality or state of being competent: such as the quality or state of having sufficient knowledge, judgment, skill, or strength (as for a particular duty or in a particular respect)

DEMONSTRATING COMPETENCE IN YOUR SUBJECT AND YOUR TEACHING

"I can learn from this person." In any learning situation, we hope to find ourselves in good hands. Nancy recalls how important the perception of competence was as she stood on the side of a mountain, ready to traverse a series of 12 ziplines. She had never done this before, and her guide appeared to be disturbingly young. But the man quickly assured her of his experience, and his calm demeanor suggested quiet confidence. The guide managed all of the gear for the group, and he and his crew repeated their safety checks at each station. An hour later, the entire group celebrated their accomplishments and expressed their gratitude to the guide for all he had done to ensure success.

Looking back, Nancy would have never hung around if the guide had appeared disorganized, inexperienced, or foolish. In fact, there's a word for it: *incompetent*. But under the guidance of a competent instructor, the entire group of inexperienced adults was able to safely reach the bottom of the mountain and enjoy the experience. There is one difference, though, between Nancy's experience and those of most students. Nancy had the ability to walk away from the situation had she perceived the instructor as incompetent. Schoolchildren don't get to do the same. So they walk away cognitively and emotionally. And in the process, they fail to learn.

Introducing Competence.

LISTEN as Doug describes the components of competence and how students think about teacher competency.

PAUSE & PONDER

Stacy Zeiger (2018) identified 10 "competencies of teachers" that are listed below. Using the "traffic light" scale, identify your strengths across these dimensions.

1. Interacting Well With Students

2. Creating a Learning Environment

3. Good at Lesson Plan Design

4. Able to Use Varied Teaching Strategies

5. Able to Assess

6. Able to Identify Student Needs

7. Good at Communication

8. Able to Collaborate

9. Maintaining a Professional Appearance

10. Demonstrating a Commitment to the Profession

COMPETENCE

We think that this is a reasonable list, but as you read this chapter, think about how students would perceive the competence of their teachers. After all, the evidence says that learning increases when students believe that their teachers are competent.

COMPETENCE DEFINED

This aspect of teacher credibility is focused on the demonstrated competence of the teacher as perceived by the student. Not surprisingly, perceived incompetence on the part of the teacher significantly undermines teacher credibility.

REFLECTIVE WRITING

Write 8–10 words that you think about when you hear the word *competence*. As you read this chapter, consider how these words apply.

Incompetent teachers "don't care about the course and/or the students" write Banfield, Richmond, and McCroskey, and

> make tests too hard, are unwilling to help students succeed, and/or present poor lectures. They may bore or confuse students, overload them with information, mispronounce words. . . . These characteristics reflect a basic lack of teaching skills. (2006, p. 63)

There's actually a name for this in communication research: *teacher misbehaviors*. There is a significant spillover effect as it relates to perceived incompetence. Teachers viewed as incompetent by students were also more likely to be viewed as untrustworthy and uncaring, even when they didn't do anything specifically to undermine relationships with students. An incompetent teacher is quickly assumed by students to be someone they should distance themselves from.

Up front, we will say that most teacher evaluation systems fail to directly address the topic of competence.

REFLECTIVE WRITING

How would your students define competence?

_____

_____

_____

_____

_____

_____

There are tools that focus on what the teacher did on some number of observations, and others that include a focus on student learning as measured on state tests. However, competence as it relates to teacher credibility is more complex than that. As we reflected on teachers in our lives, we realized that we placed them in three categories based on their competence.

The first type we identified were teachers who know their subject but have little idea how to teach it. We call these folks *walking encyclopedias*. It's no wonder that the research indicates that teacher content knowledge does not have a strong effect size. In fact, teacher subject matter knowledge has an effect size of only .23, well below the average of .40 ("250+ Influences," n.d.). Increasing teachers' knowledge but not their understanding of how to convey that knowledge does not improve student learning. Dominique remembers a teacher who really knew his history. Every fact, every date. He had stories about every chapter of the history book. But his class was chaos. The teacher talked over students' heads and assigned them chapters to read at home that were too complex. He gave pop quizzes that the majority of students failed, so he would invent a range of makeup activities loosely based on the content students were supposed to be learning. Dominique wrote a bunch of reviews of current events, even though the class was US history. Suffice it to say that nobody learned much from this course, even though the teacher knew a lot of history.

The second type we identified were teachers who really don't know their content, but they have great strategies. We call these folks *surface dwellers*. They are generalists in the worst sense of the word. They know just enough to get by, but their strategies are fantastic. Dominique remembers an art teacher who fit this category. The class was filled with activities. They worked bell-to-bell on a range of projects and tasks. But they didn't really learn anything about artistic technique, terminology, aesthetics, or critiques, which was the major content of this art history course. Dominique recalls the class being fun as well as the many conversations with peers about how they weren't learning anything but that it was "an easy A." Years later, with a spouse who teaches art history, Dominique realized that there was a lot of content he missed.

The third kind we identified were teachers who know their subject *and* know how to teach it. They are true teachers: the ones who understand their subject and how to align instructional approaches with the learning that students need to do. They are not addicted to specific strategies but rather deploy them purposefully based on the content being taught. In addition to his science teacher, Dominique remembers a math teacher who fits this category. She clearly knew her content and demonstrated her skills by modeling them each day. But she also engaged the class in problem solving and collaborative learning. She guided their thinking and did not simply assign lots of independent work. She retaught when necessary, but Dominique remembers most of the students learning the content the first time and personally doing very well in her middle school class.

To harness the power of teacher credibility, you have to know both your content and how to teach it.

REFLECTIVE WRITING

Identify a teacher in your own education who fit this description—knowledgeable about the subject and instruction. Consider the following:

- How would you describe your learning?
- What made this person so memorable?

Importantly, students know when you don't know your subject and when you aren't able to teach it effectively. And when teacher credibility declines, so does learning. There is a theory that explains this phenomenon—pedagogical content knowledge.

PEDAGOGICAL CONTENT KNOWLEDGE

Lee Shulman (1986) noted that all students need a teacher who is more than simply knowledgeable about the subject matter. He stated that students also need a teacher who can teach that subject clearly and effectively. He named his theory pedagogical content knowledge (PCK). Since then, there have been hundreds of studies demonstrating the power of this idea. Researchers have investigated the role of PCK in a wide range of subjects and grades, ranging from science (e.g., Southerland & Gess-Newsome, 1999) to physical education (e.g., Ward & Ayvazo, 2016) and reading instruction (Hurk, Houtveen, & Grift, 2017). There is no meta-analysis on this topic yet, so we do not have an effect size to report. But the evidence suggests that it is a useful construct. We believe that teachers should be knowledgeable and know how to teach the content.

The implications for this idea are twofold. First, we need to make sure that teachers know their content. That may mean that some professional learning time is focused on the content students need to learn. For example, a group of elementary school teachers were talking about their students' performance on a benchmark assessment. They noted that many of the students struggled with fluency. One of the teachers, Gil Sanzo, said, "I thought my students read fast enough to score well on this, but maybe I'm not understanding the term here and how it's assessed."

INSIDE THE CLASSROOM

Watch as this math teacher introduces a lesson to students. Consider his instructional prowess as well as his content knowledge. Are you confident that you can learn from him based on the brief visit you just made to his classroom?

Ann Buckley responded, "I think we should spend some time focused on this. I'm with you Gil, I thought this assessment was about rate. But I'm seeing other things that I'm not sure I understand. I mean, I know WCM—words correct per minute, but there are other items about their level that have me confused."

As a team, they agreed to learn more about the content, specifically what was included in the realm of fluency. And they discovered that they were missing a focus on prosody, or the use of vocal stress, intonation, pauses, inflections, emphasis, and the like. They discovered that a team developed a prosody scale for the National Assessment of Educational Progress (Daane et al., 2005) that they could use to guide their work. They also noted that Hudson, Lane, and Pullen (2005) provided a more detailed checklist of a student's prosody that they could use:

1. Student placed vocal emphasis on appropriate words.
2. Student's voice tone rose and fell at appropriate points in the text.
3. Student's inflection reflected the punctuation in the text (e.g., voice tone rose near the end of a question).
4. In narrative text with dialogue, student used appropriate vocal tone to represent characters' mental states, such as excitement, sadness, fear, or confidence.
5. Student used punctuation to pause appropriately at phrase boundaries.
6. Student used prepositional phrases to pause appropriately at phrase boundaries.
7. Student used subject-verb divisions to pause appropriately at phrase boundaries.
8. Student used conjunctions to pause appropriately at phrase boundaries. (p. 707)

"Who knew that there was so much to this idea?" Ms. Buckley said. "I'm feeling much better about what it means to be a fluent fourth-grade reader. I have to admit that I was a little skeptical about only focusing on reading speed.

"I was worried that students would lose the meaning if we kept pushing them to read faster. But I can get behind this."

But deep understanding of the content is not enough. We think of content knowledge as necessary but not sufficient. This group of teachers also needed to know how to teach fluency, and specifically prosody. Importantly, there is not one right way to teach things, but there are wrong ways. Imagine if this group of teachers decided to engage students in round robin reading, with students required to read texts aloud to the class that they have never seen before. It's not likely that this practice would increase students' overall fluency. Instead, the research evidence would suggest strategies such as repeated reading, readers' theatre, paired oral reading, and the like. Our point here is that competence, as part of teacher credibility, requires both content knowledge and pedagogical knowledge.

Teachers who have strong pedagogical content knowledge are also comfortable when they don't know something. They do not try to hide that fact from students, and they don't invent answers that may or may not be accurate. Instead, they provide honest responses to students when questions are raised for which they are not sure about the answer.

Sometimes, the questions students ask are complex, and there is not a simple answer. For example, when the students in a life science class asked why bees were dying (which they had learned about in a video), their teacher let them know that there really isn't a clear answer to this question and that scientists are trying to figure this out. It may seem obvious to answer this way, but far too often teachers compromise their credibility by answering students' questions with inaccurate or incomplete information.

Other times, students' questions are more about facts. For example, a student asked her elementary school teacher how long it would take a spaceship to get to the sun. This information was not at the tip of the teacher's tongue, nor is it really part of the content she would be expected to know. Rather than make up an answer or offer a vague answer, such as "it would take a really long time, and it depends on the speed," the teacher responded, "Now that's an interesting question and I don't know the answer to that. But, I'll look it up and find out. How about I share what I learn tomorrow?"

We have never said that the teacher needs to know everything. You need to know your content and how to teach it, but there is a lot of information and there are a lot of ideas out there in the world. Being honest with students about what you don't know, and making a commitment to find out or to acknowledge that there is not a clear answer, goes a long way toward building credibility. The remainder of this chapter focuses on knowing how to teach the content that you know effectively. We'll start with teacher clarity.

REFLECTIVE WRITING

What is unique about the content you teach?

What tools do your students need to be taught to access that content?

As you think about teacher competence, we encourage you to think about what your students need to know so that you don't waste their time focused on content they have already mastered. In addition, we encourage you to think about your own learning needs and how you will meet those needs. Doing so will build your skill set and will likely result in better outcomes for your students. Use the grid below to identify the learning your students need to do, the learning you need to do, and how you will accomplish that learning.

What are the learning needs of my students? *What do students need to learn?*	What are my learning needs so I can support my students' learning needs?	What learning will I engage in to support my learning needs? *What will I do on my own? What can I do with colleagues?*

COMPETENCE

TEACHER CLARITY
CONTRIBUTES TO YOUR COMPETENCE

THINK ALONG

Teacher Clarity. Dominique discusses the value of teacher clarity, which requires that you share learning intentions and success criteria. Why do you believe that teacher clarity is a positive contributor to competence?

With an effect size of .75, there is good reason to consider teacher clarity as an essential part of one's practice ("250+ Influences," n.d.). At a basic level, teacher clarity requires that the teacher know what students need to learn, communicate those learning intentions directly, and ensure that students know what success looks like. At a deep level, teacher clarity extends to the lucidity of the examples and guided instruction the teacher provides, and the practice students are asked to do. We will come to those parts of teacher clarity later in this chapter. For now, let's focus on the part that concerns what students need to learn.

First and foremost, we should not spend valuable instructional time on things that students have already learned. Students are frustrated when the teacher squanders time like this, and they question whether the adult can accurately gauge their strengths and needs. Thus, teacher clarity requires that you know what students already know so that you can teach in the gap between what they know and what they need to know. There are a number of tools to determine what students already know, such as initial assessments, reviews of performance on previous units, and interactions with students.

Once we know what students need to learn, we have to identify an appropriate sequence of learning. Often called learning progressions, the flow of content is an important consideration. Teachers who cannot logically sequence concepts and skills risks being viewed as scattered, and their students' perception of their competence suffers. As with many things in education, there are likely many appropriate progressions and some bad ones. We find it more effective, and time saving, to plan the sequence of learning with peers. Those planning sessions, and the resulting success with students, also contribute to the team's collective efficacy.

Once the sequence of learning has been identified, students need to know each day what they are supposed to learn and how they will know they have learned it.

REFLECTIVE WRITING

What are the benefits of students knowing what success looks like in your classroom? How might your students define success?

This learning intention (which others might call a learning target, goal, or objective) elevates the level of the students' investment in learning, as it moves them from compliance to commitment. Learning intentions are paired with success criteria. Success criteria equip students with a means for gauging their own learning. We have outlined a planning process for creating learning intentions and success criteria in the *Teacher Clarity Playbook* (Fisher, Frey, Amador, & Assof, 2018). We have included some example learning intentions and success criteria from that book in Figure 3.1.

INSIDE THE CLASSROOM

Let's take a look at several teachers' learning intentions and success criteria. What do you notice about them? Of course, writing them on the board and then ignoring them does no good. They need to be discussed with students.

Learning Intention	Success Criteria
Figure 3.1 Examples of learning intentions and success criteria	
I am learning that plants are the primary source of matter and energy in most food chains.	• I can define *source of matter* and *energy* as they relate to food chains. • I can identify producers and consumers in a food chain. • I can analyze a food chain from a given biome and identify the role that plants play.
I am learning that content on the internet must be checked for reliability and trustworthiness.	• I can use the "about" information to identify authority information. • I can use the domain name to identify credible sources (e.g., .com versus .edu or .gov). • I can rate the accuracy of the information.
I am learning to write number sentences based on the models and pictures.	• I can use words to describe the model and picture I made. • I can write a number sentence with the same meaning as the words.
I am learning to locate several ideas and details presented in a text.	• I can independently read an informational text and underline key ideas and details.

Source: Fisher, D., Frey, N., Amador, O., & Assof, J. (2019). *The teacher clarity playbook: A hands-on guide to creating learning intentions and success criteria for organized, effective instruction.* Thousand Oaks, CA: Corwin.

If there is sufficient clarity in the lesson, students will be able to answer these three questions:

- What am I learning today?
- Why am I learning this?
- How will I know that I have learned it? (Fisher, Frey, & Hattie, 2016, p. 27)

The first question focuses on the content being learned. The second question focuses on the relevance of the lesson, and we will spend more time on this topic in the next chapter on dynamism. And the third question focuses on the success criteria. Each of these is important if you want to mobilize the power of teacher clarity, not to mention increase your credibility. We suggest that you use these questions as a temperature check. Ask three to five random students these questions, and keep track of the percentage of answers that are correct. If you are teaching with clarity, students will know the answers to these questions. In knowing the answers, their sense of competence grows.

COMPETENCE REQUIRES THAT YOU ALIGN INSTRUCTIONAL EVENTS WITH THE LEARNING INTENTIONS.

We believe that students' sense of competence is underappreciated, at least in terms of its relationship to teacher competence. Yet most of us would draw a clear association between something we learned well and the person who taught it to us. When students experience an increased sense of competence in learning, they attribute it in part to the skills of the teacher. The teacher's clarity, especially in the use of learning intentions and success criteria, provides a pathway for students to become more competent. And when they see themselves as competent, you benefit as well. But simply having learning intentions and success criteria does not ensure that the lesson flows. Competence requires that you align instructional events with the learning intentions.

Check in with students about their understanding of learning expectations and success criteria. Each day for one week, ask randomly selected students these questions:

- What are you learning today?
- Why are you learning this?
- How will you know that you have learned it?

Chart the data in Week 1 on the table below. Then set a goal for yourself. Which of the three questions do you want to focus on first? What percentage growth do you want to see? Continue to collect data to see if you have reached your goals—and then set new ones.

Week	Number of students who answered Question 1 correctly	Percentage	Number of students who answered Question 2 correctly	Percentage	Number of students who answered Question 3 correctly	Percentage
1						
2						
3						
4						
5						
6						

Goals and Notes

GRADUAL RELEASE OF RESPONSIBILITY DEFINED

Nancy and Doug have been working to understand teacher moves that increase student competence and confidence for several decades. They have based their work on a theory first developed for reading comprehension instruction, the gradual release of responsibility (Pearson & Gallagher, 1983). The intent of this instructional framework is to ensure that the teacher moves from assuming "all the responsibility for performing a task . . . to a situation in which the students assume all of the responsibility" (Duke & Pearson, 2002, p. 211). As Graves and Fitzgerald (2003) note,

> Effective instruction often follows a progression in which teachers gradually do less of the work and students gradually assume increased responsibility for their learning. It is through this process of gradually assuming more and more responsibility for their learning that students become competent, independent learners. (p. 98)

The way we think about this is that there are times in a lesson in which the teacher is doing more of the work, and there are times in which the students are doing more of the work. The flow of the lesson depends on students' increased understanding, so that increased responsibility can be released. Another way of thinking about this is as a gradual increase in responsibility for students. Our interpretation of the theory has four major components (see Figure 3.2).

INSIDE THE CLASSROOM

Watch as second graders learn about solid figures. Notice the intentional moves of their teacher to ensure their learning. How does this teacher use each phase of the gradual release of responsibility to build students' confidence and competence?

Figure 3.2 The gradual release of responsibility

A Framework for Gradual Release of Responsibility

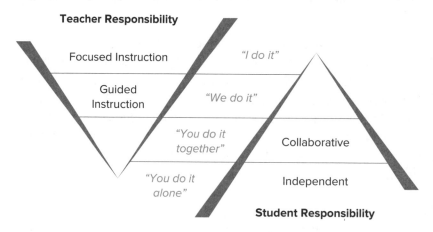

Source: Fisher, D., & Frey, N. (2014). *Better learning through structured teaching: A framework for the gradual release of responsibility* (2nd ed.). Alexandria, VA: ASCD.

As a quick overview, here is how we define each of the phases:

- **Focused instruction** is a time during which teachers establish the purpose (the learning intentions and success criteria) and model their thinking. They open up their brains and talk through their own thinking. Focused instruction is also a time for direct or explicit instruction.

- **Guided instruction** scaffolds students' understanding as their teachers use prompts, cues, and questions to address errors and misconceptions. Guided instruction can be done with the whole class, in a small group, or individually.

- **Collaborative learning** requires that students interact with their peers using academic language to share or problem solve. Students are given tasks or prompts that they likely could not complete individually, and teachers structure the interactions.

- **Independent learning** provides students with opportunities to both practice and apply what they have been taught. This can occur during class time or outside of the class.

The problem with this graphic is that people think we intend lessons to be linear. They're not. You can start at any phase, depending on what you want students to learn. For example, the students in Ellen Gordon's third-grade class came in from recess and were asked to respond to a writing prompt. That's an independent task. Next, they were invited to talk with their table partner about the question they had responded to. This is a collaborative task. As they did so, Ms. Gordon circulated around the room, skimming students' papers and listening to their conversations. She noted a pattern of errors and used that information to inform her modeling (which we call focused instruction). As she completed her modeling, she informed the students about the learning intention and success criteria (also part of focused instruction) before asking them to return to their papers and update their thinking individually. While students were revising, she asked four students to join her at her desk. These four were identified because their answers were exceptionally strong, and she wanted to push their thinking a bit more. Sometimes her small group guided instruction focuses on students who are struggling or who need additional support to be successful. Other times, as was the case in this lesson, she wanted to extend the thinking of some students so that they could support their peers when they returned to their groups. Hopefully, this quick example shows you that there is no prescribed order to the phases. It's about being intentional and ensuring that learning experiences are designed to allow students to accomplish the learning intentions and success criteria.

REFLECTIVE WRITING

What has been your experience with the gradual release of responsibility?

FOCUSED INSTRUCTION IN PRACTICE

With our colleagues Maria Grant, Diane Lapp, and Kelly Johnson, we have observed many lessons in which teachers masterfully design and deliver amazing experiences for students. One such example appeared in the *Journal of Adolescent & Adult Literacy*, and parts of that lesson are presented here. Cesar is a sixth grader whose science class is studying the pH of the oceans and its effects on marine organisms. They are addressing this content standard: "The number and types of organisms in an ecosystem depend on factors such as the amount of light, the pH of the environment, and/or the temperature range." The current lesson focuses on the pH component of this standard.

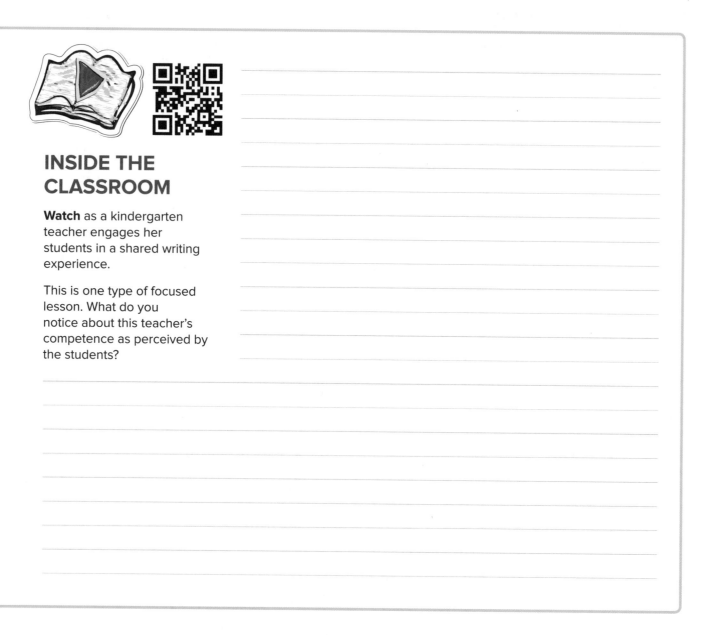

INSIDE THE CLASSROOM

Watch as a kindergarten teacher engages her students in a shared writing experience.

This is one type of focused lesson. What do you notice about this teacher's competence as perceived by the students?

As we have noted, lessons do not have to begin with purpose and modeling. Cesar's teacher, Andrew Barnett, might establish the purpose at the outset of the lesson so that students can activate their relevant background knowledge. On other days, Mr. Barnett might engage students in other components of the framework first, revealing the purpose after students have engaged in inquiry. Regardless, at some point in each lesson, modeling and purpose setting support students' developing academic background knowledge, or what a person knows about content related to other school disciplines.

Mr. Barnett begins with a short video about the acidity of the oceans. After viewing it, students share their thoughts with a partner by responding to teacher-posed questions designed to stimulate inquiry: *What does current research seem to show about the relationship between acidic water and global warming? What next steps might you and your partner take to investigate this further?* Through viewing the video and sharing partner talk, students activate and build background knowledge like real-world scientists banking new understandings. Mr. Barnett is able to gauge what they know and need to know, thus contributing to his ability to meet their needs—a crucial dimension of competence.

While the vast majority of scientists agree that ocean acidification appears to be correlated with increased carbon dioxide emissions, there is another perspective on the issue.

REFLECTIVE WRITING

What quality indictors do you look for during focused instruction?

What advice do you have for new teachers regarding focused instruction?

Keeping the methods of inquiry in mind, Mr. Barnett includes readings and podcasts that discuss the skeptics' views of the claim that ocean acidification is caused by excessive carbon dioxide introduction into the oceans. Multiple perspectives on any issue should be considered as a part of the investigation model of thinking. For example, some people think that the oceans are large enough to buffer the carbon dioxide that is being dissolved into the water. Mr. Barnett wants his students to investigate all sides of this issue. In conveying the nuances of this knowledge, Mr. Barnett signals to his students that his knowledge of the topic is deep. Mr. Barnett now poses the learning intention for this lesson: *to investigate the decrease in the number of organisms with shells in the ocean due to increased ocean acidity*. Upon reading this intention, students would understand that they are focusing on why there are fewer animals and plants in the oceans today.

Mr. Barnett models his thinking through a think-aloud about how he makes connections between content resources. When students hear how an expert thinks, they are better able to build vocabulary, access prior knowledge, and fill in gaps in background knowledge. In addition, they have further exposure to his expertise. He says,

> I noticed that the video showed lots of ways that carbon dioxide gas is put into the atmosphere—burning gas, driving cars, factories releasing carbon dioxide into the atmosphere. I wonder where all that gas goes? When I read the excerpt from the book about oceans, I learned that ocean acidification is caused by the absorption of carbon by the oceans. I remember that when we studied corals, we learned that organisms that have shells, like corals, can't survive in water that is too acidic. I'm thinking that there must be a connection between our air pollution and the survival of animals and plants in the ocean. Maybe it has something to do with ocean acidification. I'd like to test these ideas.

The figure below contains a number of indicators regarding student interaction and engagement during focused instruction.

- Use this as a checklist when you plan a lesson.
- Video record this aspect of your lesson, and see which of these were experienced by students.
- Optional: Invite a trusted colleague into your classroom to observe.
- Optional: Together with colleagues, watch a video from the internet, and practice using this tool.

	Teacher to Student	Student to Student	Student to Content

Focus Lesson
 I do it
	☐ Teacher explicitly states the learning intention(s) for lesson.
	
	 ☐ Teacher restates learning intention(s) throughout lesson.
	
	 ☐ Teacher models process and context for thinking.
	
	 ☐ Teacher invites students to join and attend to modeling.
	
	 ☐ Teacher poses convergent questions for student response (seeking answer).
	
	 ☐ Teacher poses divergent question for student response (questions without specific answer).
	
	 ☐ Student behavior reflects cognitive interaction and engagement.
	
	 ☐ Teacher revisits other phases of gradual release.
		☐ Students explain their reasoning to each other.
		
		 ☐ Student conversation builds on responses of others.
		
		 ☐ Students talk to partner about a posed question and explain thinking to each other.
		
		 ☐ Students explore others' thinking and reasoning through
		     Restating
		     Paraphrasing
		     Questioning
		
		 ☐ Students continually try to reclarify thinking by explaining reasoning in multiple ways.
			☐ Students demonstrate background knowledge.
			
			 ☐ Students communicate the intended learning intention(s) in their own words.
			
			 ☐ Students take notes.
			
			 ☐ Students record using graphic organizer.

COMPETENCE

THINK ALONG

Collaborative Learning. Dominique shares some experiences with collaborative learning. What lessons can you learn from these experiences? How can you ensure that your students have opportunities to collaborate with their peers?

A few days later, Mr. Barnett begins the lesson with group work. Collaborative learning provides students the opportunity to put their knowledge into action. When scientists solve problems, they use their own data in conjunction with the data and ideas of others to develop solutions.

The challenge of productive group work is the demand on background knowledge. To address this, Mr. Barnett starts with groups of three or four students searching the internet for information about pH using *internet reciprocal teaching* (Castek, Coiro, Leu, & Hartman, 2015), in which students question, summarize, predict, and clarify the texts that they find. With peer support and a familiar instructional routine, students can build their background knowledge and then activate it in subsequent inquiry lessons or reading tasks. Mr. Barnett has curated reliable digital resources for his science students to utilize, rather than simply turning them loose on the internet and hoping for the best. Again, his students benefit from his competence as a knowledgeable teacher. In turn, they experience success in deepening their own knowledge about the topic.

REFLECTIVE WRITING

What quality indicators do you look for when you use collaborative learning in your classroom? What advice do you have for new teachers regarding collaborative learning?

PAUSE & PONDER

The figure below contains a number of indicators regarding student interaction and engagement during collaborative learning.

- Use this as a checklist when you plan a lesson.
- Video record this aspect of your lesson, and see which of these were experienced by students.
- Optional: Invite a trusted colleague into your classroom to observe.
- Optional: Invite a colleague to watch a video from the internet with you and practice with this tool.

	Teacher to Student	Student to Student	Student to Content
Collaborative *You do it together*	☐ Teacher provides a challenging collaborative task for students to apply and extend learning. ☐ Teacher poses a challenging problem, task, or situation for students with which to grapple. ☐ Teacher holds students individually accountable for contributing to the learning. ☐ Teacher revisits other phases of gradual release.	☐ Students work in small groups of not more than five students. ☐ Students facilitate each other's learning. ☐ Students dialog about ideas. ☐ Students participate in content talk using academic language. ☐ Supported with sentence frames/ structures ☐ Not supported by sentence frames/ structures ☐ Students make inferences and explain reasonableness through evidence. ☐ Students explain their options/ opinions they thought about and why they chose certain options/ opinions. ☐ Students justify their reasoning by using multiple models or data.	☐ Students are collecting, recording, and interpreting. ☐ Students utilize previously learned concepts in a new/emerging way. ☐ Students interact with concepts without a guaranteed outcome (building meaning).

GUIDED INSTRUCTION IN PRACTICE

Most students benefit greatly from an apprenticeship-like thinking experience, in which the teacher guides them to become more expert in a cognitive task. Once Mr. Barnett has used a think-aloud to model how he considers the parameters of a science problem, he supports the students' inquiry by asking them to plan for an experiment that will test the effects of increasing acidity on the material that composes most shells of marine organisms, calcium carbonate. To scaffold this activity, he provides a template for inquiry thinking that includes built-in mechanisms for collegial conversations (see Figure 3.3). Students generate inquiry plans using the guide sheet template. Like real scientists, they can consider new perspectives, revise ideas, and construct new knowledge in a meaningful, lasting manner.

He monitors student progress by moving around the room, listening in on conversations between partners. His next steps are dependent on his on-the-spot analysis of what each student needs. Consider, for example, how Mr. Barnett responds when Cesar told his partner that he wanted to investigate how acid affects calcium carbonate:

> I want to drop a solution with a pH of 7 on a piece of calcium carbonate shell. Then I'll observe what happens. If nothing happens, I'll try a solution with a pH of 8 on the same piece of shell. I'll continue this by increasing the pH of the solution that I drop on the shell. I'll keep observing and will record my observations.

Hearing this conversation, he strategically asks Cesar about the numbers on the pH scale by saying, "Which numbers on the pH scale represent acids?"

REFLECTIVE WRITING

What quality indicators do you look for when you use guided instruction in your classroom? What advice do you have for new teachers regarding guided instruction?

_____

_____

_____

_____

_____

_____

_____

Figure 3.3 Template to guide students through the inquiry process

Area of Focus	My Ideas	My Partner's Ideas	Our Ideas (after our discussion)
Before the Investigation/Experiment			
What question do you want to study?			
What evidence would you want to look for in order to study your question?			
How will you record your evidence or data? (Design a chart or data table to hold your evidence.)			
After the Investigation/Experiment			
What does your data tell you?			
How do your ideas connect with the ideas of others in your class? How do your ideas connect with those of other scientists studying the same concepts?			
What are your conclusions? Record your conclusions by writing two or three paragraphs. Be sure that your ideas are based on your evidence/data.			

Source: Grant, M., Lapp, D., Fisher, D., Johnson, K., & Frey, N. (2012). Purposeful instruction: Mixing up the "I," "we," and "you." *Journal of Adolescent & Adult Literacy, 56,* 45–55.

If Cesar was not able to respond satisfactorily, Mr. Barnett could offer a physical cue by pointing to the pH chart on the wall or in the textbook as a reference. Cesar would hopefully be able to note that solutions with a pH below 7, not above 7, are acidic. Before Mr. Barnett resorts to *direct explanation,* he should give Cesar the chance to dig into his store of background knowledge by offering a prompt or cue (Figure 3.4). *Prompts* are statements or comments provided by a teacher to guide students to think about prior learning or experiences. *Cues* are suggestions that help students shift their attention to what is relevant and important to their understanding. If Mr. Barnett asks a question intended to help Cesar recall that a pH value below 7 indicates that the solution is acidic, he is prompting. If he points to a pH chart, he is offering a cue. Both methods of guided instruction help to move Cesar along the learning continuum toward more expert content thinking. It is critical to note that Mr. Barnett's role in the guided instruction component of the GRR is essential. This is the phase in which students benefit most from the teacher's ability not merely to correct, but to notice what misconceptions or partial understandings might be confounding the student.

REFLECTIVE WRITING

What common student misconceptions do you regularly encounter?

What instructional responses do you use?

What is the relationship between anticipating student misconceptions and pedagogical content knowledge?

Figure 3.4 Ways that the teacher might offer prompts and cues in response to particular misunderstandings expressed by a student

What Student Might Say	How Teacher Might Respond
I want to drop a solution with a pH of 7 on a piece of calcium carbonate shell. Then I'll observe what happens. If nothing happens, I'll try a solution with a pH of 8 on the same piece of shell. I'll continue this by increasing the pH of the solution that I drop on the shell.	Teacher might ask, "Which numbers on the pH scale represent acids?" (a prompt to help student recall prior knowledge)
The solutions that have pH numbers that are above 7 are acids.	Teacher might say, "Let's take a look at the pH chart in your textbook. What does this tell us about the pH of acids?" (a cue to help direct the student's attention to the correct content information).
I don't understand this chart. Aren't pH numbers under 7 bases?	Teacher might say, "Let's review the chart together. Solutions, like vinegar and lemon juice, that are acids have pH values that are below 7. This means that acids have pH values below 7. Bases, like ammonia, which you use sometimes for housecleaning, have pH values above 7. Ammonia has a pH above 7. Bases have pH values above 7. Now can you try to explain the chart and pH to me?" (Direct explanation is used if prompts and cues are not adequate.)

Source: Grant, M., Lapp, D., Fisher, D., Johnson, K., & Frey, N. (2012). Purposeful instruction: Mixing up the "I," "we," and "you." *Journal of Adolescent & Adult Literacy, 56,* 45–55.

PAUSE & PONDER

The figure below contains a number of indicators of student interaction and engagement during guided instruction.

- Use this as a checklist when you plan a lesson.

- Video record this aspect of your lesson, and see which of these were experience by students.

- Optional: Invite a trusted colleague into your classroom to observe.

- Optional: Invite a colleague to watch a video from the internet with you and practice with this tool.

	Teacher to Student	Student to Student	Student to Content
Guided Instruction *We do it*	☐ Teacher poses question and asks partners to think, share, answer, and justify their thinking. ☐ Teacher supports students to develop thinking through Prompts Cues Convergent questions Divergent questions Direct explanation (after prompts and cues) ☐ Teacher questions students to uncover misconceptions. ☐ Teacher assists students to clarify their thinking. ☐ Teacher revisits other phases of gradual release.	☐ Students explain their reasoning to each other. ☐ Student conversation builds on responses of others. ☐ Students talk to partner about a posed question and explain thinking to each other. ☐ Students explore other students' thinking and reasoning through Restating Paraphrasing Questioning ☐ Students continually try to reclarify thinking by explaining reasoning in multiple ways.	☐ Students are collecting, recording, and interpreting. ☐ Student tasks are visible and directly reflect the purpose in Reading Writing (pictures, words, numbers) Conversation Solving problems ☐ Students consolidate understanding about concepts they are learning (synthesizing, building learning).

INDEPENDENT LEARNING IN PRACTICE

In order for students to truly internalize science concepts and content, they must wrestle with ideas in a way that allows them to negotiate personal meaning. The day after students conducted their experiments, Mr. Barnett offered them a new reading for their individual consideration. For this lesson, students read an article entitled "New Ocean Acidification Study Shows Added Danger to Already Struggling Coral" and then were asked to interpret the content by integrating article ideas with previous learning. Helping students further negotiate meaning and incorporate ideas, Mr. Barnett assigned a RAFT writing task (Santa & Havens, 1995) in which students independently demonstrated their understanding of the inquiry process as it related to the target content. Creating RAFTs encourages writing from multiple perspectives.

RAFT stands for

> R = role (Who is the writer; what is the role of the writer?)
>
> A = audience (To whom are you writing?)
>
> F = format (What format should the writing be in?)
>
> T = topic (What are you writing about?)

After reading the article, students respond to the RAFT as follows:

> R = sea urchin
>
> A = marine life
>
> F = letter
>
> T = how acidification affects building my shells

In addition to being an effective way to assess students' understanding of the content, RAFTs are helpful in providing differentiation. Teachers can modify the role, audience, format, or topic to match the literacy strengths of groups of students. Consider how the following RAFTs would each meet the needs of a diverse group of students in Cesar's class:

R =	researcher
A =	scuba divers
F =	list
T =	three reasons why acidification is threatening

R =	reporter
A =	Florida residents
F =	public service announcement
T =	a new danger to reefs and coral

R =	scientist
A =	journal readers
F =	science journal article
T =	why organisms are susceptible to predation and damage

With new knowledge from the learning experiences planned by their teachers, students are well prepared to document their understandings of the demise of the reefs off the Florida coast and the relationship to ocean acidification in a creative, relevant form. Reading these, Mr. Barnett should be able to get a sense of who has gained a deep understanding of the concepts of ocean acidification, as seen through a lens of inquiry, and who, perhaps, needs more support.

REFLECTIVE WRITING

What quality indicators do you look for when you use independent tasks in your classroom? What advice do you have for new teachers regarding independent tasks?

The figure below contains a number of indicators regarding student interaction and engagement during independent learning.

- Use this as a checklist when you plan a lesson.
- Video record this aspect of your lesson, and see which of these were experienced by students.
- Optional: Invite a trusted colleague into your classroom to observe.
- Optional: Invite a colleague to watch a video from the internet with you and practice with this tool.

	Teacher to Student	Student to Student	Student to Content
Independent Learning *You do it alone*	☐ Teacher confers with students to Assess understanding Monitor progress ☐ Teacher elects to revisit other phases of gradual release. ☐ Teacher establishes purpose for independent work. ☐ Teacher holds students accountable for independent work.	(Not applicable)	☐ Students reflect on own learning. ☐ Students are collecting, recording, and interpreting. ☐ Students function independently. ☐ Students can manage the task independently Reading Writing (pictures, words, numbers) Conversation Solving problems

COLLECTIVE EFFICACY AND COMPETENCE

Source credibility influences the decisions we make about what we will take action on versus what will be disregarded. A team member who is viewed as a competent teacher is able to influence the group about educational practices. Perceived competence by the group is an important dimension in the social perception of the group. Further, a team that believes it is composed of competent members is confident in its ability to accomplish tasks.

However, competence alone is not sufficient when it comes to the collective efficacy of the group. As noted in Chapter 1, the "independent contractor" is a metaphor for a competent colleague who is a team member in name only. Her energy is invested almost exclusively in refining her own practice, and she is not professionally generous in sharing ideas or opening her classroom to others. She is a social loafer, allowing others to pull the weight of the team, while she contributes comparatively little to the work. Other members of the department or team are left to wonder about her formula for success. We believe this feeds the "born to teach" mythology in the profession.

A colleague who is perceived as incompetent is at risk of becoming increasingly isolated. In fact, a colleague who is viewed as incompetent by students will soon be viewed similarly by fellow teachers. The result can be increased avoidance and distancing by the others in the group. It isn't easy to place oneself in the classroom of a team member who is struggling with students who may be questioning the teacher's competence. But investment in the relationship with the struggling colleague can be a lifeline. Team support is crucial and can alter the trajectory of this teacher's credibility. All of us recall times in our lives when someone didn't give up on us. The professional generosity we extend to a troubled member contributes to the collective efficacy of the group, because it speaks to the beliefs we hold about our capacity to affect positive change.

> A COLLEAGUE WHO IS PERCEIVED AS INCOMPETENT IS AT RISK OF BECOMING INCREASINGLY ISOLATED.

CONCLUDING THOUGHTS ABOUT COMPETENCE

Teaching is a complex endeavor. It's more than knowing stuff or knowing a couple of good strategies. Effective teachers are seen as competent by their students, which requires that teachers have both content knowledge and instructional skills. Together, they are powerful and contribute to teacher credibility. Unfortunately, a lot of professional learning focuses on isolated strategies rather than the deep knowledge required of the content and the tools useful to ensure that students learn that content. But now we know more and can change that. In doing so, we will elevate our credibility with students and perhaps even build or reinforce our collective efficacy, which in turn will help students learn more and better.

Nancy provides you with a challenge to conclude this chapter. In essence, she suggests that you invite a colleague into your classroom to explore the link between teaching and learning and the ways in which students perceive competence. In doing so, you are also likely to have mastery experiences and provide your colleague with modeling, which will contribute to your collective efficacy.

CHAPTER 3 CHALLENGE

Invite a colleague into your classroom to explore perceptions of competence.

DYNAMISM

noun | dy · na · mism | \ ˈdī-nə-ˌmi-zəm \

A dynamic or expansionist quality; the *dynamism* of a natural leader

HARNESSING THE POWER OF DYNAMISM

"There was this teacher. . . ." How many of us have said that when asked why we joined this most noble profession? Doug remembers two teachers, both named Jan, who were passionate about their students' learning. These two men taught together and advised many student clubs. Their classrooms (history and English) were vibrant and exciting, and it seemed as if there was always something new to learn from them. They were passionate and dynamic. Their energy was palpable. They dressed in togas when we read *The Odyssey*. They turned the lights down, played soft music, and read by flashlight for the short story "A Rose for Emily." They cried when they read *Faithful Elephants*. They debated ideas openly with each other. Almost all the teachers we have met talk about teachers who inspired them.

But what about people who do not become teachers? Are they similarly inspired? We have lost count of the number of times some professional is giving a speech and acknowledges a teacher. What was it about that teacher that was so powerful? It was probably a combination of things, including the fact that the teacher saw something in you that you didn't see in yourself, at least not yet. And it probably was the passion the teacher had for the content, your learning, and the whole field of education. When we think about dynamism as part of teacher credibility, we think of teachers who

- are energetic and vibrant,
- seem to enjoy teaching and learning,
- are passionate about education as a profession, and
- exude self-confidence.

Introducing Dynamism.

LISTEN as Doug describes dynamism.

PAUSE & PONDER

Using the "traffic light" scale, identify your strengths in the area of dynamism. As you think about each of these dimensions, ask yourself, "Would my colleagues and students describe me as . . . ?"

	My colleagues' perceptions	**My students' perceptions**
1. Energetic and vibrant.		
2. Enjoying teaching and learning.		
3. Passionate about education as a profession.		
4. Exuding confidence.		

Remember, teacher credibility is in the eyes of the student. And remember that your colleagues will want you to be part of the team if they see you as credible with students.

PAUSE & PONDER

How did you rate yourself?

What do you think as you see this information presented visually?

Is there a gap between your colleagues' perceptions and your students'?

DYNAMISM DEFINED

Sometimes, when we talk about this aspect of teacher credibility, people tell us that they are shy, or that this is not their personality. Of course, there is a range of expression when it comes to dynamism, but some level of passion is required if we are going to ensure student learning. Wangberg (1996) argues that there are at least four ways to demonstrate passion in the classroom. He notes that "the best teachers are people who are passionate about their subject *and* passionate about sharing that subject with others" (p. 199). Interestingly, he is an insect biologist and college professor who wrote a children's book, *Do Bees Sneeze? And Other Questions Kids Ask About Bugs* (Fulcrum, 1997). No offense to our colleague and science teacher Cody O'Connell who loves insects, but it's kind of hard to make bugs interesting to most people. If you can make insects interesting, it seems like anything could be made interesting. Wangberg says that teachers need to consider the following four actions if they want to harness the power of passion:

1. Enthusiasm
2. Immersion in the subject
3. Creative and innovative approaches
4. The teacher as a learner

Some level of passion is required if we are going to ensure student learning.
iStock.com/SDI Productions

PAUSE & PONDER

What motivates you to learn something new? You are an adult and you teach children, and we recognize the difference therein. We just think it's valuable to think about our own motivations to learn, as we're sure that they are different from our students' motivations. Teachers who are highly invested in their practice not only embrace learning for themselves but see possibilities for how they might apply their new learning in their classrooms. The table below lists some items from the Programme for the International Assessment of Adult Competencies (PIAAC), specifically the program's readiness-to-learn items. Take a look at each item, and decide how much impact it has on your interest in learning.

Item	On a scale of 1 to 5, with one being the lowest level of motivation and 5 being the highest, what is the impact of each item?				
When I hear or read about new ideas, I try to relate them to real-life situations to which they might apply.	①	②	③	④	⑤
I like learning new things.	①	②	③	④	⑤
When I come across something new, I try to relate it to what I already know.	①	②	③	④	⑤
I like to get to the bottom of difficult things.	①	②	③	④	⑤
I like to figure out how different ideas fit together.	①	②	③	④	⑤
If I don't understand something, I look for additional information to make it clearer.	①	②	③	④	⑤

Source: Gorges, J., Maehler, D. B., Koch, T., & Offerhaus, J. (2016). Who likes to learn new things: Measuring adult motivation to learn with PIAAC data from 21 countries. *Large-Scale Assessments in Education*, *4*(9). https://doi.org/10.1186/s40536-016-0024-4

What patterns do you notice about yourself? How might this help you? How might a dynamic teacher change your perceptions and readiness to learn?

DYNAMISM

DYNAMISM THROUGH ENTHUSIASM

This is arguably the most commonly considered factor in passionate teaching. Teachers who are excited, and display that excitement for students, can motivate learning. Of course, we've all experienced the teacher who went overboard with this and we became skeptical. But a level of excitement about the content is useful. As it is often said, enthusiasm can be contagious, and that is probably a good thing for students.

There are a number of ways to demonstrate enthusiasm, including the tone in your voice, the emotional stories you tell, or the presentation techniques you use. Regardless of the approach, students should know that you care about the content. Doug often says that the first thing on a teacher job description should be to make content interesting. If you can accomplish that, you're halfway there. And by the way, recall that an aspect of trustworthiness is your commitment to your content. It is easier for the instruction to stick when you care about the subject and you show it.

Young children seem to always be excited about their learning. First-grade teacher Maria Torres was introducing a writing task to her students and said, "Today, we're going to write about the books we've been reading. Remember that we've focused on life in the city and life in the country and how it's different. Today, you are going to write about those differences."

THE FIRST THING ON A TEACHER JOB DESCRIPTION SHOULD BE TO MAKE CONTENT INTERESTING.

Several students said "Yeah!" while Michael blurted out "I knew it!" and Bianca said, "I know exactly what to write!" Ms. Torres then told students that she would be giving them some extra supplies, including chart paper and markers to brainstorm. They practically cheered. By the time they were released to start writing, the excitement was palpable, and they were ready to go.

Teachers of older students have to work a little harder. We're not sure why, but the excitement of learning wanes as students get older. Jenkins (2015) notes that the level of enthusiasm for school is highest in kindergarten, at 95%, and lowest in Grade 9, at 37% (and there is a slight climb in 12th grade, to 45%, for the students who remain in school). Collier (2015) noted, "Nearly half of students in Gallup's 2014 student poll report being either not engaged (28 percent) or actively disengaged (19 percent) in school. The poll of 825,000 fifth- through 12th-graders shows a clear slide as children progress in school" (p. 58). We have to change that if we want students to learn more effectively.

REFLECTIVE WRITING

The statistics on student disengagement are sobering. How do you reengage students in your classroom? What signs do you look for to signal disengagement?

History teacher Joanna Schaefer dresses up in costumes on certain days to teach history. She has arrived at school in a toga, a World War I soldier's uniform, a coal miner's outfit, and a host of other getups. She has the personality to pull this off, and her students love it. Romel, one of her students, said, "She's really serious about the history, and she wants us to experience it. It's cool that she takes this much time to be ready for the lessons." We're not suggesting that you have to dress up for class; it's just one way that a teacher found to demonstrate enthusiasm for her high school students.

Middle school science teacher Andrew Jacobs pumps his students up in advance of each lab. He talks about the labs with vigor and ensures that his students know that the lessons are all designed to get them ready for the labs. And on lab days, he wears his lab coat and exudes confidence and a heartfelt commitment to the discipline. For example, when his class was dissecting sheep hearts, Mr. Jacobs said, "It's really exciting to be able to look inside an actual organ and see all of the things that we've been reading and learning about. You get to be surgeons today, and that means we're respectful of each other and the animal that is allowing us to learn. I know I'm really pumped about this, but I want to go slowly so that I can really see all the things we've learned about. Are you ready?" The students immediately put their goggles on and got to work.

INSIDE THE CLASSROOM

As you watch this second grade teacher, think about his enthusiasm for his content and his students. He is clearly delighted and humored by his students' responses.

How does this compare to classes that you observe?

What can you learn from this teacher about enthusiasm?

DYNAMISM THROUGH IMMERSION IN THE SUBJECT

The second area that Wangberg (1996) described as a pathway to passion involves a deep knowledge of the subject as well as a commitment to, and love for, that subject. We've already discussed the value of knowing your subject in the chapter on competence, so we'll focus on the commitment to that subject. One way that we think about this aspect is that that subject exudes from you, and you can't help it. It's just part of who you are, and it is clear that you love every minute of studying it. Wangberg says he thinks about this as if the teacher were covered (both metaphorically and literally) by the media he or she has been using. Doug remembers a math teacher who had blue marker all over his fingers from writing on the overhead projector. He was physically covered with his content and didn't even seem to notice.

Fourth-grade teacher Gretchen Fleming loves poetry and writing; everyone knows it. She has a poem a day that she recites from memory for her students. Every day, a different poem. At some point each day, Ms. Fleming will close her eyes and say, "Students, gather round. It's time." And she will close her eyes and recite a poem. She invites students to talk about the poem and what it means. She recites it again, this time with her eyes open, making eye contact with various students who seem to need that message today. She then invites any students who "have a poem in their pocket" to share. Some recite from memory while others read from a scrap of paper, literally taken from their pocket. Some read the works of others, and some read their own creations. As Sean said, "I thought I hated poetry. Now, I can't imagine the day without it."

ONE WAY THAT WE THINK ABOUT DYNAMISM IS THAT THAT SUBJECT EXUDES FROM YOU, AND YOU CAN'T HELP IT. IT'S JUST PART OF WHO YOU ARE.

We were talking with a noneducator friend about this, and she recounted an experience that shaped her life. She said, "There was this professor who loved computer programming. Everyone fought to get in his class, even though the pass rate wasn't very good, because the content was really hard. He was in the lab all of the time ready to help. He would talk code to anyone who would listen. It was as if it was the most important thing in the world. I ended up changing my major to study more with him, and I'm a programmer today because of it. And I met my husband at work. My life was changed because one person was so immersed in his subject and I wanted to know more."

Survey your students (anonymously, of course), asking them what they believe you love about your subject. Collect their responses and cluster them into themes. Are they correct? Do you need to convey other passions about the subject for your students?

DYNAMISM THROUGH CREATIVE AND INNOVATIVE APPROACHES

The third area that Wangberg (1996) identified as a possible way to demonstrate passion involves the instructional approaches that are used to convey the content. We can all remember really boring approaches to content delivery that demotivated us, even if the subject was pretty interesting. And hopefully we remember some really interesting ways that teachers used to engage us in learning.

INSIDE THE CLASSROOM

Several teachers share their innovations on this video. They are not suggesting that you replicate their ideas. But notice the excitement they convey.

What innovations do you want to try with your students?

Before we delve too much deeper into this area, we should restate one of our core beliefs, and that is that teachers should never hold an instructional strategy in higher esteem than their students' learning. In other words, if the strategy does not work, change it. We all have our favorite strategies, but if they are not ensuring learning for a certain group of students, it is our responsibility to make a change.

Another core belief we share is that the approaches we use with students should have some evidence of impact. We are not saying that they have to have published studies or meta-analyses behind them, although those are good things. Students are not our proverbial guinea pigs, and yet teachers should feel free to innovate. That innovation should be based on information that the ideas are likely to work. We're not saying that all innovations will succeed, but they can lead to new insights and increased engagement.

The second-grade team at Parkview Elementary was discussing their lessons on gravity and how they were not sure that students were really understanding the concept. As Amanda Strauss remarked, "They're supposed to know that objects will fall to the ground unless something holds them up. But I don't think that they're getting it. We've read about it and demonstrated it, but do they get the concept? I'm not sure."

TEACHERS SHOULD NEVER HOLD AN INSTRUCTIONAL STRATEGY IN HIGHER ESTEEM THAN THEIR STUDENTS' LEARNING. IF THE STRATEGY DOES NOT WORK, CHANGE IT.

Susan Forr responded, "Yep, I agree. And I'm not sure what we should do about it. We did the same thing last year and it really seemed to work. I think we need some new ideas with this group of students. I mean some are getting it, but really, most are not."

As a team, they decided to reengage the students in demonstrations, but rather than talk through them, they would ask students to predict what would happen and why. They collected a wide range of items, such as a hammer, a ball, and a pen. The teachers also decided that they would put some barriers in the way so that some of the objects would not fall to the ground. That way, they theorized, students would understand that an object will fall unless something holds it up.

Ms. Forr said to the team, "We've got to act like we're not sure what will happen and then go a little overboard with excitement. We want them to really focus on these concepts."

They also found several videos, including one entitled "What is Weightlessness?" produced by the Public Broadcasting Service that they would use to further students' understanding. Ms. Strauss noted, "I think we need to be a bit creative with this, and maybe the students talking on this video will help. They're a little older than our students, and it might motivate them." The team agreed to develop a performance assessment and a writing prompt to determine whether their additions to the unit made a difference.

The actions of the second-grade team at Parkview Elementary may seem commonplace, but some groups of teachers do not believe that they have permission to augment the approved lessons and textbooks. Their innovations were not that extreme, and they felt comfortable making changes in students' experiences to ensure learning. In doing so, their passion shined through.

A more significant example occurred in a ninth-grade English class. The teacher, Wayne Chen, noted that his students were not engaged in reading. In fact, several of his students said that they had not read a book on their own since early elementary school. Mr. Chen knew that assigning a whole class novel would not ensure that his students actually read it.

REFLECTIVE WRITING

What is a memorable approach you use in your classroom?

So, he decided to get creative. He asked his students what they wanted to know more about. He asked them about the questions they had in life. Each class generated a set of questions that were of interest to them. Mr. Chen then created a ballot for each class and invited students to vote on their first, second, and third choices of questions. He told them that the top choice would be the focus of the class for the current month, and then, depending on whether or not the students valued the experience, the next question could be the focus for the following month. The winning questions by period were as follows:

- Avenge or forgive? (first period)
- Does age matter? (second period)
- What is race, and does race matter? (third period)
- Can you buy your way to happiness? (fourth period)

Using these questions, Mr. Chen worked with the library media specialist to generate a list of books, about 20 titles long, for each question. Some of the books were edgy and required parent permission. Some were less or more complex. There was a range of titles for each question. Mr. Chen then introduced the lists to his students and invited them to make choices. He told them that they would form book clubs and meet during class time to talk about their books. He also told them that he would read a book to them that was not on the list. And, by the end of the month, they would have a response to the question they had voted on. As he noted, "This was a big risk for me. I had to give away a lot of control. And I took a risk with the titles on the list. But it was really worth it. I saw students reading their books in the front office, waiting to get picked up. I heard them talking about their books during discussions. And, their written responses showed me that they were really reading and thinking about the question."

DYNAMISM THROUGH TEACHER AS LEARNER

GOOD TEACHERS CONTINUE TO BE STUDENTS.

There is a reason that the phrase "lifelong learner" is so popular in schools. As Wangberg (1996) notes, "Good teachers continue to be students," (p. 199), which is the final way that passion can be demonstrated for students. Teachers continue to learn from a variety of sources, including from their peers during professional learning opportunities, from published research, from professional books, from workshops and seminars, from personal learning networks, from online resources, from designing new courses and curriculum, and from solving problems, making mistakes, and reflecting on those experiences.

We believe that the reason Wangberg included this as part of passion was because learning new things keeps us fresh. We are professionals, and professionals keep learning. And when we learn, we want to try out ideas with our students. When those ideas are new, or hold potential to impact learning, we're enthused, and it shows. Kindergarten teacher Tricia Logan told her students that she was going back to school to learn more about being a teacher. Her students were shocked.

"Why do you gotta go back to school?" Sivanathan asked.

"Because learning is great," Ms. Logan said,

> and I can't wait to learn new things so I can share them with you. Every time I come to your class after I have school, I'll wear my school shirt. See this shirt I'm wearing? It's from my school. When I wear this shirt, you can ask me about my school and what I learned. It's just like visitors to our classroom like to ask you what you are learning, why you are learning that, and how you'll know you learned it. You can ask me those same questions.

Fifth-grade teacher Gabriela Camerino is part of a book club that reads young adult literature. Ms. Camerino's students know about her club because she regularly shares book titles with her students, talking about what the others in her group said. During one such session, Ms. Camerino said,

> Okay, so I've been waiting to share this book for a few weeks. You know how much I like learning about new books and then sharing them with you. But this one, I had to keep it for myself first. I loved this book. It was so special. It touched my heart. I can't tell you much without ruining it for you, but this character Merci is a pretty special kid. And the book won a big award for excellence. I know that the library has 10 copies right now, so if you're interested, stop by there and get it quickly before other people find out. You know, I'm going to tell everyone to read *Merci Suárez Changes Gears* (Medina, 2018).

There are a number of ways to engage your learning and maintain your passion. When you do so, your students will likely notice, even if you don't tell them directly.

PAUSE & PONDER

The final gift from Wangberg (1996) is his Passion Inventory (see Figure 4.1). We found this tool to be useful as a reflection guide. It will help you assess your current level of dynamism and might point to some things that you can do to increase your score, and then perhaps your students' learning. Take the Passion Inventory.

Figure 4.1 Passion Inventory

Score one point for each item that depicts you or your students.

☐ I am enthusiastic about my teaching. It is something I enjoy and look forward to doing. It is a fun, exciting, and stimulating activity for me.

☐ My students can sense my enthusiasm. They have conveyed this impression to me in their evaluations or in their personal comments.

☐ I am continuing to learn. I am active in research. I read and attempt to keep up with the appropriate literature. I obtain new information from my students.

☐ My students are witnesses to my interest in learning. They see me doing research, reading the literature, conversing with colleagues, participating in professional conferences, and actively engaging with my discipline.

☐ I can get absorbed in my work, but not so self-absorbed that others are excluded. I am likely to share what interests me and bring my interests to the attention of others.

☐ I continue to try new approaches in my teaching. The class that I have taught several times is different and better than when I began. Sometimes I try things that do not work, but these failures do not prevent me from taking new risks or experimenting with my teaching.

☐ I care about my students. I want them to learn, to realize their potential, and to succeed in class and in other useful and challenging endeavors.

Your Score:

7 pts. Powerfully passionate!

6 pts. Pridefully passionate

5 pts. Pretty passionate

<5 pts. Seek help from a passion professional!

Source: Wangberg, J. K. (1996). Teaching with a passion. *American Entomologist, 42,* 199–200.

DYNAMISM

PAUSE & PONDER

What surprises you about the results? Where do you see areas for growth? Who will you need to enlist to support your growth?

STUDENT PERSPECTIVES ON RELEVANT LEARNING EXPERIENCES

THINK ALONG

Making Learning Relevant.
Dominique shares his thinking related to relevance. What makes learning relevant for you? Did you have anything in common with Dominique?

"Why do we need to learn this?" "Will it be on the test?" "Who will ever need to know this?" How frustrating for teachers to be confronted with these questions. After all, they are in school and supposed to be learning. True, but the fact is that student motivation matters. Bribing and manipulating students isn't the answer to motivation. Motivation comes, in part, when the learner sees the task as relevant. Parenthetically, motivation also increases when students feel that they can be successful. The expectancy-value model of learning (Wigfield & Eccles, 2000) suggests that students are more likely to be engaged in school if they expect they can do well and if they value the learning that schools provide. And, there are tools that you can use to determine students' expectancy-value.

A sample tool used to determine students' expectancy-value-cost can be found in Figure 4.2. Notice that the sample, applied to mathematics and science learning, includes three types of items. Some are labeled with an E, which relates to the *expectations* students have for themselves and the class. Others are labeled with a V, which relates to the *value* students place on the item. And the third type of items are labeled with a C, which focuses on the *cost* students attribute to the experience.

Administer the survey on the next page anonymously to your students. Calculate the averages for each of three aspects: *expectations, value,* and *cost.* Complete the table below:

Factor	Average Score	Initial Thoughts About the Data
Expectations		
Value		
Cost		

Now, engage in a bit of thinking about the data. Use the tool "My Notes for Data Analysis" (following Figure 4.2) to explore your thinking about students' motivation. What actions does this inspire? Are you willing to share this with a colleague and develop plans to change students' expectations, the value they have for the content, and the cost they believe they will pay for this experience?

Figure 4.2 Expectancy-Value-Cost Scale

Item	Strongly disagree (1)	Disagree (2)	Slightly disagree (3)	Slightly agree (4)	Agree (5)	Strongly agree (6)
I know I can learn the material in my [math or science] class. (E1)	①	②	③	④	⑤	⑥
I believe that I can be successful in my [math or science] class. (E2)	①	②	③	④	⑤	⑥
I am confident that I can understand the material in my [math or science] class. (E3)	①	②	③	④	⑤	⑥
I think my [math or science] class is important. (V1)	①	②	③	④	⑤	⑥
I value my [math or science] class. (V2)	①	②	③	④	⑤	⑥
I think my [math or science] class is useful. (V3)	①	②	③	④	⑤	⑥
My [math or science] classwork requires too much time. (C1)	①	②	③	④	⑤	⑥
Because of other things that I do, I don't have time to put into my [math or science] class. (C2)	①	②	③	④	⑤	⑥
I'm unable to put in the time needed to do well in my [math or science] class. (C3)	①	②	③	④	⑤	⑥
I have to give up too much to do well in my [math or science] class. (C4)	①	②	③	④	⑤	⑥

Source: Kosovich, J. J., Hulleman, C. S., Barron, K. E., & Getty, S. (2015). A practical measure of student motivation: Establishing validity evidence for the expectancy-value-cost scale in middle school. *The Journal of Early Adolescence*, 35(5–6), 790–816.

DYNAMISM

My Notes for Data Analysis

Questions	My Thoughts
Step 1: What parts of these data catch my attention? Just the facts.	
Step 2: What do the data tell me? What do the data NOT tell me?	
Step 3: What good news is there to celebrate?	
Step 4: What are possible common challenges suggested by the data?	
Step 5: What are my key conclusions?	
Step 6: What actions could I take to impact the data in a positive direction?	

INCREASING RELEVANCE FOR STUDENTS

To our thinking, relevance can be established at least three ways.

Learning Outside These Walls

One way that we see teachers increase the relevance is to help their students see the value of the learning for their lives outside the walls of the classroom. We are not fans of saying to students "in the real world," because we believe that school *is* the real world for students. We don't imagine going there, whether physically or online. We actually go there. Instead, we like to frame this as an opportunity for students to consider the things they will need to know and be able to do outside of the classroom. We do caution you to consider how distant you make the connection. Telling a fourth grader that she will need this in college is probably a bridge too far. However, telling her that improving her writing will help her convince people of things that she wants them to do might just do the trick.

Two examples come to mind. A high school geometry teacher, teaching about midsegments of triangles, says to her students, "This is how volcanologists measure volcanoes. So, if you're interested in that profession, you'll really need to know this." Honestly, there isn't a big calling for volcanologists, but when you are 15 years old, it sounds cool. Later in the lesson, this teacher says, "If you are creating props for a play, you'll want to know this so you can make them in correct proportion, and your audience doesn't look at the set and think that there's something wrong."

Second-grade teacher Kristen Davis said to her students, "We're learning about solid figures. We want to know their names and their parts, such as edges, bases, and vertices. We want to know this because our family and friends will know what we're talking about when we say the soup can is a cylinder, but the box of cereal is a rectangular prism. And really, when you are putting new toys together, adults say things like the base or the vertices, and we'll all know what they're talking about."

Learning About Yourself

Sometimes relevance comes because students are provided an opportunity to learn about themselves.

All of us find this highly relevant. Dominique was thrilled to learn that there is not just one writing process as he was taught in school, but rather that we have internalized processes for writing that are influenced by the audience, format, and topic. Learning about his writing process was highly motivating.

When Earl Herman's students are preparing for a debate, he reminds them, "This is an opportunity to learn about yourself. You'll get a chance to really think about what you believe. And it will help you figure out how you can win an argument. Really, this is useful outside of this class. Maybe you want to convince a friend

REFLECTIVE WRITING

How can you make your content increasingly relevant for students? Have you considered the various ways to ensure that students see their experiences as valuable?

of something, or maybe you want to have a reasonable disagreement with your parents. Debates are not fights. They're reasoned discussions about issues with evidence and claims. Good debaters get their way more often, and you might like that."

Educated People Know Stuff

The final way that we see teachers establish the relevance of the lesson is to convince students that the content is inherently worth knowing. For some, this is a stretch, but we have seen it work. Our ah-ha moment was when a high school teacher said to her students, "Look, pretty soon you're going to get to vote. And you might vote on my health care or retirement funds. So, it's really important to me that you're informed so that you can make good decisions. Ready?"

When we asked Jennifer Nielson's fifth graders about why they were learning about the American Revolution, their answers tended to focus in this arena. One student said, "You know, if you don't know history, you'll make mistakes later. Like you'll have to repeat it and suffer." Another said, "Who wants to be the person who doesn't know stuff?" And another said, "It's like basic things you have to know. It's how our country got created. Like everyone should know that."

"WHO WANTS TO BE THE PERSON WHO DOESN'T KNOW STUFF?"

Relevance matters, and more often than not, teachers need to ensure that students see relevance in their learning. Sure, there are some topics that are so riveting that students want to know everything about them. And there are individual passion projects that one student, or a small group of students, want to know about. We have a friend whose third-grade son will read anything, and we mean anything, related to the *Titanic*. For some reason, he's fascinated with it and devours everything on the topic. Unfortunately for him, there is more to learn about than the *Titanic*. His teacher used his absorption with the *Titanic* when possible, but also knew that she had to expand his interest base and make other things compelling. Which brings us to the tasks we assign students.

PAUSE & PONDER

The figure below, from the *Teacher Clarity Playbook* (Fisher, Frey, Amador, & Assof, 2018) contains several learning intentions. In addition, it provides two or three options for ensuring that the learning is relevant for students. As you read these, consider which of the options is better and why. Record your selections in the final column of the figure and your thoughts on the page that follows. Talk with colleagues about the best options for making learning relevant for students. In doing so, you are likely to increase your students' perception of your dynamism.

Learning Intention	Relevance	Which is better?
Partition shapes into parts with equal areas.	1. You will need this on the upcoming test. 2. When we make fractional parts, we want to be fair and have each part the same size.	
Identify reliable and trustworthy content from the internet.	1. Doing so makes sure that you are not a victim of crimes or lies. 2. If you know what is trustworthy, you become a critical consumer of information.	
Ask questions about unknown words in a text.	1. Readers work to make meaning of the texts they read. 2. Asking questions helps you pay attention to what the author is saying. 3. When you find unknown words, you can add them to your vocabulary journal.	
Identify the impact of water pollution on the environment.	1. When you understand the causes and impact, you can help contribute to a healthy environment. 2. This unit will prepare you for the next one, when we study the water cycle.	
Describe how artists use tints and shades in painting.	1. These are important words that you should know and be able to use on your own. 2. These concepts help you understand artistic style so that you can discuss art with others.	
Given a specific plate boundary (subduction zones, divergent margins, and transform margins), predict the resulting geological features.	1. This will help when you go to buy a house so that you are not buying near a dangerous area. 2. This is another opportunity for us to develop our predictive skills. 3. You will do better on the state test if you know this content.	

PAUSE & PONDER

My notes about my choices:

BORING INDEPENDENT TASKS

One of the most effective ways we have found to crush dynamism is to hand students a worksheet and ask them to complete it. As Marcia Tate (2015) notes, "Worksheets don't grow dendrites" (p. 1). Doug is prone to calling worksheets "shut-up sheets," because most of them are effective in keeping students quiet and busy, but not learning much. Instead, as we noted in Chapter 3, students need to engage in a variety of tasks, assignments, and activities that deepen their understanding.

But Jennifer Gonzalez, in her blog *The Cult of Pedagogy,* provided us a different way to think about the seemingly endless photocopies and workbook pages that teachers use. She developed the worksheet continuum (see Figure 4.3). This helped us have conversations about more appropriate tools and less appropriate tools, rather than simply saying that all worksheets are bad.

Notice that there are several recommendations toward the "powersheet" end of the continuum. These are likely more useful for students and will probably not harm the dynamism in your classroom. Also, we do believe that students need some skills practice, and we agree with Gonzalez that it should not count for a grade. We like to remind ourselves that practice does not make perfect; practice makes permanent. Of course, students need more than practice; they also need to apply, but that's another topic. For now, we'll stay focused on the use of *powersheets,* as Gonzalez calls them, and provide two examples.

Figure 4.3 Worksheet Continuum

THE WORKSHEET CONTINUUM

BUSYSHEET
Keeps kids busy but has little educational value

POWERSHEET
Directly supports learning: may support other tasks

word searches word scrambles irrelevant coloring, cutting, and pasting	recall questions comprehension questions labeling stuff	skills practice (only as needed and not for a grade)	graphic organizers note-taking templates data collection tools planning sheets

Source: Gonazalez, J. "Frickin' Packets." *The Cult of Pedagogy*, 26 Mar. 2018. https://www.cultofpedagogy.com/busysheets/.

INSIDE THE CLASSROOM

Interactive graphic organizers are one type of powersheet. Watch as students create their 3-D tools and engage with their peers to collect information and ideas.

How are these different from photocopied worksheets?

The students in Becky Palmer's third-grade class are learning about animal adaptation. They have a wide range of reading materials and internet sites that they can use in their search. Ms. Palmer has created a data collection tool, so her students know what to focus on. They need to identify the habitat, the animal(s), and the adaptation specific for the environment. This powersheet is useful, because students use it as a recording device rather than a final product. Over time, they will need to generalize about animal adaptation and write about their learnings. In addition, each group will be provided a specific animal to learn more about such that they can create a presentation for the class.

The students in Ray Huggins's science class are studying states of matter. Mr. Huggins uses Foldables that were developed by Dinah Zike (www.dinah.com). Foldables are a type of graphic organizer that students manipulate with their hands and minds. They are multidimensional and often colorful. Students cut, fold, and glue as they transform information and learn. You don't have to purchase Foldables—they are an innovation that any teacher can use with her students to help them interact meaningfully with ideas and information.

The students in Mr. Huggins's class created an envelope fold (see Figure 4.4) and labeled it with the four states of matter. They took notes inside each of the flaps. In doing so, they develop schema and practice recalling the information. They are also typically proud of what they make and like to use these tools to study. Marlene said, "I thought that they were kinda silly at first, but they really help you. I remember way more this year at this school because the teachers don't just copy things for us to memorize. We have to create it, and then we can remember it."

REFLECTIVE WRITING

How do you enliven independent learning in your classroom?

Figure 4.4   An envelope fold for the four states of matter

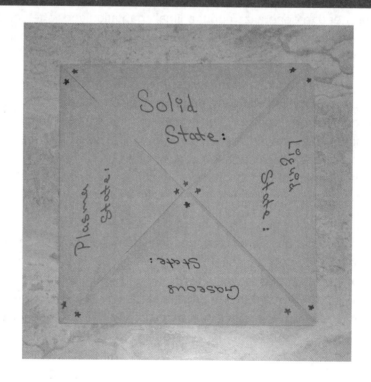

VISUALS AND PRESENTATIONS

Let us be blunt. Most digital slide decks should be trashed. They're undermining your dynamism. Students spend time looking at slide after slide with way too many words and try desperately to write down everything on the slide in a futile attempt to learn something. It's frustrating and boring. We aren't saying to stop using slide decks, but rather, use them to enhance your dynamism.

Several years ago, Doug was presenting at a big conference. Following the session, a woman approached him and said, "I don't want you to take offense at this, but your presentation is way better than your slides. In fact, the slides detracted from your presentation. I hope you hear this as I intend, but I really hope you'll read *Presentation Zen* (Reynolds, 2008). I think it will change your life."

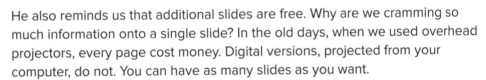

MOST DIGITAL SLIDE DECKS SHOULD BE TRASHED.

And it did. As Reynolds points out, too often we attempt to have our presentations do two things—serve as the handout and the slide. He calls them *slideuments*. He argues that we should separate these two. There are documents to be distributed to learners and slides that complement what the speaker is saying. A simple but powerful idea when you think about it.

He also reminds us that additional slides are free. Why are we cramming so much information onto a single slide? In the old days, when we used overhead projectors, every page cost money. Digital versions, projected from your computer, do not. You can have as many slides as you want.

His book (now in its second edition) focuses on design features useful for all of us. He notes the value of images that directly relate to what you are saying. As he notes, the focus should be on the speaker, not the slides. When there is critical information to be projected, we should pause for students to read it, or read it to them. We should never say "I know that this is too small for you to see." What a waste!

In addition, Reynolds reminds us that we should use words on slides sparingly. He also says that the font size and type can change so that key ideas are emphasized. There is a lot more that we can say about the design of presentation materials, but that's really beyond the scope of this book. Suffice it to say that we should all consider our slides, and make sure that they are not dampening the dynamism in the classroom. Instead, they should contribute to the excitement and relevance of the learning experience. It is worth the time to invest in good presentation materials, because it conveys a message to students. And that message is multifaceted, from how much I care about your learning based on how much time I put into the presentation to how interesting I think the content is. Can you tell we're converts?

REFLECTIVE WRITING

Honestly assess your audiovisual tools.

Are they contributing to your dynamism or detracting from it?

COLLECTIVE EFFICACY AND DYNAMISM

Your enthusiasm, immersion in the subject, creative and innovative approaches, and investment in yourself as a learner communicate volumes about your value as a team member. On the other hand, a person who approaches a complex team goal with little appetite for the task will not inspire the group. Moreover, a pessimistic prediction of the group's success potential can negatively influence group performance (Barsade, Ward, Turner, & Sonnenfeld, 2000). We need to be quite clear here. Multiple perspectives, including negative ones, are of great value to the group. In fact, disagreement about approaches is often necessary, especially in disrupting the echo chamber effect that is a product of group thinking. High-functioning teams with a strong sense of collective efficacy seek out opinions different from their own and interrogate counterclaims carefully before making high-stakes decisions. But a member with unwavering pessimistic beliefs about his or her team is likely to be uncooperative, thus sparking conflict within the team.

It is important to note that a team member with an optimistic view of the team, but a pessimistic view of students, can also diminish the efficacy of the group. Consider "the talker" who we described in the first chapter. This team member values colleagues but is reluctant to follow through with team decisions about the common challenge in a meaningful way.

A PESSIMISTIC PREDICTION OF THE GROUP'S SUCCESS POTENTIAL CAN NEGATIVELY INFLUENCE GROUP PERFORMANCE.

This dilutes the data the team can draw upon to examine the impact of their instruction. In addition, this team member's covert resistance compromises the team's ability to monitor and modify their plan. Instead, the team may be forced into a simplistic binary decision: "Well, that didn't work. Let's get rid of that and move on." The team is robbed of its ability to reflect and revise, two essential practices for continuous improvement. The talker's lack of teacher credibility, including a low level of dynamism with students, has a ripple effect on the team's collective efficacy. Indeed, her lack of enthusiasm for her students and investment in herself as a professional is apparent to her students, and it compromises the team's collective efforts.

REFLECTIVE WRITING

There is an incredible amount of brainpower we can capitalize on when we take our individual capacity and contribute it to a collective whole. How can you use your efficacy to contribute to the belief that you and your team can impact each and every student?

_____

_____

_____

_____

_____

_____

_____

_____

_____

_____

_____

CONCLUDING THOUGHTS ABOUT DYNAMISM

Let's not forget the line from Shakespeare's _Julius Caesar_, "Passion, I see, is catching." When you display your passion for your subject and your students and you make learning relevant, you harness the power of dynamism. It's only part of the overall teacher credibility effect, but it sure seems important in this highly distracted society. After all, we're competing with YouTube, Fortnight, Snapchat, and a host of other distractions for our students' attention. And without their attention, it's hard for our lessons to make a difference. When we have their attention, and they believe that they can learn from us, great things happen.

Nancy provides you with a challenge to conclude this chapter. In essence, she asks,

> How can you demonstrate your passion and dynamism?

> Without going over the top, how can you increase this aspect of your teaching such that you are dynamic in the eyes of your students and in the eyes of your colleagues?

How can you
demonstrate your
passion and dynamism?

IMMEDIACY

noun | im·me·di·a·cy | \ i-ˈmē-dē-ə-sē\

a. The quality or state of being immediate

b. Something that is immediate—usually used in plural

ATTENDING TO IMMEDIACY

The final area of teacher credibility focuses on the perceived, and even actual, distance between the teacher and his or her students. We hope you have all had an experience in which you felt close to a teacher. This closeness is known as immediacy. This shouldn't be confused with misplaced advice about teachers being friends with students, but rather that teachers are relatable and accessible. Dominique recalls a teacher from middle school who always seemed to know what to say to make people feel comfortable. The environment he created was safe for learning, and the language, both verbal and nonverbal, was humane and growth producing. He came across as authentic, or, as Dominique would have said at the time, real. Students could relate to him. They thought of him as an ally and mentor. Students did not misbehave in his class because of the relationship they had with this teacher. We say that as a reminder that the four aspects of teacher credibility are interwoven. But those same students who behaved so well in this teacher's class acted out in other classes. As you can imagine, there were many factors that went into the success of this teacher and the learning that his students did. But in this chapter, we'll focus on the perception of closeness that the students had.

Introducing Immediacy.

LISTEN as Doug discusses immediacy, or the idea that students believe that they are close to their teachers.

Using the "traffic light" scale, identify your strengths in the nonverbal area of immediacy. As you think about each of these dimensions, ask yourself, "Would my students describe me as . . . ?"

I move around all areas of my classroom.

I make a point of using eye contact with students.

I am intentional about using friendly facial expressions.

I smile and laugh frequently.

What are you noticing about the patterns in your responses? Are there areas that you'd like to change? As you read this chapter, think about the ways in which students perceive you based on the closeness they perceive, both physical and metaphorical.

IMMEDIACY

IMMEDIACY DEFINED

The concept of immediacy was introduced by social psychologist Albert Mehrabian (1971), who noted that "people are drawn toward persons and things they like, evaluate highly, and prefer; and they avoid or move away from things they dislike, evaluate negatively, or do not prefer" (p. 1).

REFLECTIVE WRITING

How does Mehrabian's quote sit with you?

Do you find this to be true in your personal and professional life?

Mehrabian explained that humans engage in both approach and avoidance behaviors often based on the perceived distance between people. Further, Andersen (1979) noted that teacher immediacy was highly predictive of teacher effectiveness, at least as perceived by students and classroom observers.

In terms of education-specific applications of Mehrabian's principle of immediacy, Velez and Cano (2008) were among the first to explore the issue as it relates to student motivation. They note the value of verbal and nonverbal cues in conveying value and importance, as well as connectiveness, to students. They also stated that high levels of teacher immediacy are correlated with increases in student motivation. In their words,

> The concept of nonverbal immediacy is based on the idea that teacher nonverbal behavior will promote feelings of arousal, liking, pleasure, and dominance. These feelings are mediated through actions such as eye contact, body position, physical proximity, personal touch, and body movement. (p. 1)

HIGH LEVELS OF TEACHER IMMEDIACY ARE CORRELATED WITH INCREASES IN STUDENT MOTIVATION.

Since then, there have been numerous studies on immediacy in the classroom. For example, Frymier and Thompson (1992) studied college students to create a model of immediacy in the classroom. Further, Baringer and McCroskey (2000) found that immediacy was a two-way street, and "Teachers who perceived their students to be more nonverbally immediate with them in their classrooms expressed more positive affect for the students than did teachers who perceived their students as engaging in less nonverbally immediate behaviors" (p. 178). Immediacy also accelerates learning with an effect size of .66, above the average of .40 identified by Hattie (2009).

IMMEDIACY

MEASURING IMMEDIACY

If you are interested in assessing your immediacy, Richmond, McCroskey, and Johnson (2003) developed a nonverbal immediacy scale (see Figure 5.1). This can be used as a self-assessment to identify potential areas of strength or need. It can also be used as a tool for others to use to provide perspective. The perspective can be that of students or other visitors to the classroom. We suggest starting with the self-assessment and deciding what you might want to update in the classroom and then, following the change, use the tool to understand the perspective of others. The tool provides a total score (and you can set personal goals to raise your score by increasing some behaviors and reducing others).

NOTES

Figure 5.1 Nonverbal Immediacy Self-Report Scale

Directions: The following statements describe the ways some people behave while talking with or to others. Please indicate in the space at the left of each item the degree to which you believe the statement applies TO YOU. Please use the following 5-point scale:

1 = Never; 2 = Rarely; 3 = Occasionally; 4 = Often; 5 = Very Often

_____ 1. I use my hands and arms to gesture while talking to people.

_____ 2. I touch others on the shoulder or arm while talking to them.

_____ 3. I use a monotone or dull voice while talking to people.

_____ 4. I look over or away from others while talking to them.

_____ 5. I move away from others when they touch me while we are talking.

_____ 6. I have a relaxed body position when I talk to people.

_____ 7. I frown while talking to people.

_____ 8. I avoid eye contact while talking to people.

_____ 9. I have a tense body position while talking to people.

_____ 10. I sit close or stand close to people while talking with them.

_____ 11. My voice is monotonous or dull when I talk to people.

_____ 12. I use a variety of vocal expressions when I talk to people.

_____ 13. I gesture when I talk to people.

_____ 14. I am animated when I talk to people.

_____ 15. I have a bland facial expression when I talk to people.

_____ 16. I move closer to people when I talk to them.

_____ 17. I look directly at people while talking to them.

_____ 18. I am stiff when I talk to people.

_____ 19. I have a lot of vocal variety when I talk to people.

_____ 20. I avoid gesturing while I am talking to people.

_____ 21. I lean toward people when I talk to them.

_____ 22. I maintain eye contact with people when I talk to them.

_____ 23. I try not to sit or stand close to people when I talk with them.

_____ 24. I lean away from people when I talk to them.

_____ 25. I smile when I talk to people.

_____ 26. I avoid touching people when I talk to them.

Scoring for NIS-S:

Step 1. Start with a score of 78. Add the scores from the following items:

1, 2, 6, 10, 12, 13, 14, 16, 17, 19, 21, 22, and 25.

Step 2. Add the scores from the following items:

3, 4, 5, 7, 8, 9, 11, 15, 18, 20, 23, 24, and 26.

Total Score = Step 1 minus Step 2.

Virginia, P., Richmond, J., McCroskey, C., & Johnson, A. D. (2003). Development of the nonverbal immediacy scale (NIS): Measures of self- and other-perceived nonverbal immediacy. *Communication Quarterly, 51*(4), 504–517. (p. 509). Used with permission.

Video record yourself, and select a five-minute segment to review. Use the Nonverbal Immediacy Self-Report Scale to analyze your performance.

What did you notice? What are your strengths? What are growth opportunities?

How did the immediacy self-assessment make you feel? What actions will you take based on the data?

Physical education teacher at Pacific Trails Elementary School Stacey Bergstrom used the self-assessment to identify areas of potential growth. As she noted,

> I see a lot of students every day as a 'specials' teacher. And I only see my students twice a week. So, I have to work really hard on my closeness with students. I heard about immediacy and thought that it might help with my relationships, so I took the self-assessment.

Ms. Bergstrom analyzed her results to identify areas that she wanted to reinforce and areas where she wanted to grow. More specifically, she identified areas in which she scored herself a 5 and compared that with areas that were lower and analyzed the questions that subtracted from her overall score.

Her areas of strength focused on her voice. She does not use a monotone voice and has a lot of vocal inflection. She also noted that many of her nonverbal behaviors were strong, but that she rarely got physically close to her students. As she said,

> We're always moving around and I'm trying to watch, coach, supervise, keep everyone safe . . . there's a lot going on. So, I don't think I get that close to students, and that may be what I need to change.

Ms. Bergstrom also said,

> I'm not really comfortable touching students. I know that's common in some schools, but it's really not the culture here, and it's not my style. So, I'm going to leave that for now. I feel like if I took that on it would be strange to suddenly have me put my hand on a kid's shoulder or something. I would rather work on some of the other areas.

We'll return to the issue of physical contact later. Our point in sharing Ms. Bergstrom's story is that she was reflective enough to consider the role of immediacy as a potential pathway to engage her students. She was willing to make a change to improve the outcomes for her students. We have tremendous respect for teachers who are willing to continue to reflect and grow. Having said that, there are a lot of general actions we can take to improve the immediacy our students experience.

IMMEDIACY

INSIDE THE CLASSROOM

What examples did you see of immediacy? Which techniques might you try?

An important area of teacher credibility focuses on the perceived, and even actual, distance between the teacher and his or her students.

iStock.com/Wavebreakmedia

Consider the following examples of general things you can do to ensure that your students feel close to you:

- Gesture when talking to the class.
- Look at the class and smile while talking.
- Circulate around the room.
- Call students by name.
- Use "we" and "us" to refer to the class.
- Invite students to provide feedback.
- Use vocal variety (pauses, inflections, stress, emphasis) when talking to the class.

In addition to those general actions you can take, there are some specific recommendations for maximizing or optimizing your immediacy.

IMMEDIACY CAN PROVIDE STUDENTS ACCESS TO THE CONTENT AND REDUCE THEIR ANXIETY, APPREHENSION, AND COMPLAINTS WHILE INCREASING THEIR FEELING OF BEING SUPPORTED.

The National Communication Association (Hess, n.d.) identified effective instructional practices that were useful in creating immediacy. While their focus is on college students, we think that their recommendations stand up in the preK–12 context. The organization states, "The positive relational messages immediacy expresses can reduce students' social anxiety that can interfere with their cognitive processing of class content" (p. 3). They also note that immediacy cannot compensate for a bad lesson, which we discussed in the chapter on competence. Instead, immediacy can provide students access to the content and reduce their anxiety, apprehension, and complaints while increasing their feeling of being supported (e.g., Kelly, Rice, Wyatt, Ducking, & Denton, 2015). So, here are their general recommendations:

1. **Take advantage of the time before class starts**. This is an ideal time to talk with students individually and let them know you know them. You can share personal stories or make connections with them about their interests. You can get physically closer to students and greet them individually. Geometry teacher Rachael McIntyre takes advantage of the passing periods between classes to stand in the doorway of her classroom. She greets every student, looks them in the eye, calls them by name, and asks them a question or makes a comment. For example, when Mohammed entered the room, she asked about his basketball game the previous evening. He had told her about it the day before, and he looked very pleased that she remembered. As Cynthia entered the room, Ms. McIntyre asked about student government and if they had made a decision about the theme for the winter dance. As Cynthia remarked later, "Ms. McIntyre always seems to know stuff about us. It's like she's right there with us even when we're not in her class."

But this is not limited to middle and high school teachers. Second-grade teacher Patty Cole maximizes her recess supervision to build immediacy with students. As she said, "I used to dread supervision. Now I love it. I get to talk with my students and watch them play. When we line up, I talk with them about things like sharing or what I noticed in a game. I use this time to make sure that my students know that I care and that I am there with them."

THINK ALONG

Greetings. Dominique discusses greetings and then physical barriers. As you listened, what came to mind? Are there barriers in your classroom that might impede immediacy?

2. **Get rid of barriers between yourself and your students**. This is probably more of a problem as students get older. It's hard to imagine a kindergarten teacher sitting at her desk, or standing at a podium, lecturing to students. But think about the physical barriers that are in place in a secondary classroom. Sometimes desks get in the way. Sometimes it's the presentation equipment. Returning to that kindergarten classroom, consider the difference between sitting in a rocking chair surrounded by students for a read aloud versus sitting in the corner using the document camera. The technology is appealing but, in this case, the result was increased distance and barriers between the teacher and her students.

One of the ways to remove barriers is to walk around the room rather than standing at a fixed place to deliver information for students. Science teacher Stanley Jones was excited when a smartboard was installed in his classroom. He knew that he could increase the range of audiovisual information used in his class. The problem was that he was practically glued to the smartboard, which created a barrier between him and his students.

REFLECTIVE WRITING

Study your proximity patterns, or invite a colleague into your classroom to note where you travel in the room. In your reflection or discussion, make sure to note where students who struggle with school are seated.

_____

_____

_____

_____

_____

_____

_____

_____

_____

_____

_____

_____

In fact, their scores on the chapter assessment were the lowest for the entire semester. But that all changed when he received a tablet that allowed him to manipulate the board from any place in the room. As Mr. Jones said, "I was so stoked with the possibilities of the technology and I didn't even think about the distance I was creating. What a difference. The levels of student engagement dropped big time. Luckily, the tech coordinator noticed and offered me a solution."

3. **Use immediacy behaviors in class discussion to facilitate better outcomes**. As we noted in the chapter on competence, student-to-student interaction is an important part of quality instruction. In fact, using classroom discussion is one of the ways that teachers can accelerate learning, as it has an above-average impact on learning (Hattie, 2009). But sometimes class discussions can be difficult to manage, especially when student responses are incorrect or even offensive. When these situations arise, remember the general tools presented earlier in the chapter. In addition, work to ensure that the environment is safe for everyone, and redirect conversations that go astray.

Sometimes there are students who are reluctant to speak in front of the whole class. Luis Mavo recognizes the ideas of students without requiring that they share in front of the whole class. As his students are engaged in conversations, Mr. Mavo walks around the room listening. He identifies powerful quotes from students and records them on his paper, attributing the quote to a specific student. When the discussion ends, Mr. Mavo displays his notes on the document camera and reads the comments from his students. Over time, they realize that their teacher believes that they have good ideas and begin to share on their own.

To ensure that she does not dominate the discussion in her classroom, high school English teacher Lisa Whitfield uses a copy of her seating chart to track student interactions. She wants to resist the urge to comment after each student response, and instead allow student discussion to emerge. She draws lines between the students who talk with each other. For example, when Maria responded to Adam, she drew a line between those students. Then, when Christine extended the comment made by Maria, she drew a line from Maria to Christine. At the end of the discussion, Ms. Whitfield shows the students the patterns of their conversations and asks them to reflect on what they see. Following one such experience, Seth said, "It seems like Michael and Ashanta talked to each other a lot. There are a lot of lines between them. Maybe more of us need to jump in the conversation."

INSIDE THE CLASSROOM

How does this teacher use principles of immediacy during her interactive read aloud? What verbal and nonverbal techniques does she use?

4. **Use immediacy to make lectures more engaging**. The National Communications Association focused on lectures, given their attention to college classes. We think this applies to most whole class instructional events, including read-alouds, direct instruction, explanations, demonstrations, and of course lectures.

The general guidelines noted above apply to this category as well. But when you are "on the stage" as the expert, which should not consume the majority of your instructional minutes, remember that you temporarily reduce your students' sense of closeness to you. In fact, these instructional events are important in the learning lives of students. But we need to ensure that students maintain their sense of closeness to the teacher when the teacher is sharing new information, especially when the content is challenging. The students in Robyn Conyers's fifth-grade class were learning about the water cycle, and Ms. Conyers was sharing an informational text with her students. Ms. Conyers knew that the information was dense and yet important. Before sharing the text with them, she said, "This is a really interesting article about water and the process it goes through. It's a little complex, so we're probably going to have to read it a few times to really get it. I'll share my thinking to get us started."

WE'RE NOT LOOKING FOR OVER-THE-TOP PERFORMERS OR "PHONIES," AS THE STUDENTS LIKE TO SAY. EFFORTS TO BUILD IMMEDIACY NEED TO BE NATURAL AND NOT CONTRIVED.

Ms. Conyers then started reading, pausing periodically to share her thinking about the text with students. As she did so, she moved around the room, pausing to make eye contact with several students. She also bent down near the desks of some students as added emphasis. When she finished her first read through the text, she said, "Whew. That's tough, but it's interesting. I didn't know a lot about water before I became a teacher. I just thought it came out of the faucet. We'll know so much more when we finish this unit. Now, could you turn to your partner and tell that person one thing that surprised you in this article?"

The lesson continued, and Ms. Conyers' students gained more information from this complex text. They did not feel intimidated by the difficulty they were experiencing, in large part because their teacher was metaphorically and physically close to them as they struggled. They trusted her, and her actions during this particular lesson reinforced their belief that they were together in pursuit of this knowledge.

5. **Keep your immediacy appropriate and natural**. The last recommendation from the National Communications Association is a good reminder that anything can be overdone, including immediacy. We're not looking for over-the-top performers or "phonies," as the students like to say. Efforts to build immediacy need to be natural and not contrived. We've all been around a person whose eye contact makes us uncomfortable or a person whose gestures are a distraction. Don't let that become you, because your efforts to increase immediacy will not have the desired impact and may actually make things worse. We're also reminded to go slowly on this one. Your students are used to a certain style from

you, and they value predictability. If you radically change your style, it will be noticed, and you'll probably be thought of as the weirdo rather than an ally. Take your time, and thoughtfully increase your immediacy with students. And then next year, remember that the first day of school is a great opportunity to start out on the right foot.

In addition to the recommendations noted above, there are a few additional areas we'd like to highlight. These include proximity, vulnerability, and touch. These three factors can also be used to improve students' perception of closeness to their teachers.

REFLECTIVE WRITING

How will you optimize your immediacy? Talk with others about how they will take action.

The physical presence of the teacher in the classroom is a powerful motivator. We know that teachers use proximity as a classroom management tool. Proximity also communicates value to students and the idea that they are psychologically close to the teacher. Teachers stand more often near students who perform well, students with whom they have a strong relationship. They also use proximity temporarily as a control when students are in trouble behaviorally. However, they consistently distance themselves from students they perceive as low achievers, albeit subconsciously (Good, 1987). When teachers change their proximity patterns, student learning can be positively impacted. Remember the physical education teacher profiled earlier in this chapter who decided that she needed to be closer to her students? There's good evidence to support her decision (e.g., Ormond & Kiechle, 1999), and it's not just limited to physical education (Sills-Briegel, 1996). Being at a close distance to students reinforces the idea that there is closeness in social and emotional ways as well.

WHEN TEACHERS CHANGE THEIR PROXIMITY PATTERNS, STUDENT LEARNING CAN BE POSITIVELY IMPACTED.

We have already talked about the need for teachers to move around the room so that they can be physically close to different students at different points in the lesson. As noted in the Teacher Expectations and Student Achievement (TESA) staff development program of the Los Angeles County Office of Education (2002), teachers are much less likely to stand near students who are low achieving. In fact, their data suggest that teachers actively avoid students they perceive to be lower performing or hard to teach. And they note, when teachers change their proximity patterns, student achievement increases.

In 1987, Thomas Good published his review of two decades of research on teacher expectations, and he showed that students the teacher perceived to be lower achieving

- Get less wait time.
- Are criticized more often for failure.
- Are praised less frequently.
- Receive less feedback.
- Are called on less often.
- Are seated further away from the teacher.
- Have less eye contact from the teacher.
- Have fewer friendly interactions with the teacher.
- Have their ideas accepted less often.

REFLECTIVE WRITING

Review the list of teacher expectations identified by Good. Which one of these could you change immediately?

_____

_____

_____

_____

_____

_____

_____

_____

_____

_____

_____

_____

_____

_____

_____

_____

_____

_____

_____

_____

_____

_____

_____

In more recent updates and reviews (e.g., Good & Lavigne, 2018), the findings are essentially the same. Teachers are not that supportive of students who struggle, and in time, these students' failure becomes a self-fulfilling prophecy (Good, Sterzinger, & Lavigne, 2018). Immediacy is a problem, but it is something that can be addressed with intentionality. In addition to moving around the classroom, teachers should consider the seating patterns that they use.

In terms of seating patterns, lower-achieving students are typically placed (or are allowed to sit) in the back of the room or in the corners. On the other hand, students who have stronger relationships with the teacher are often found in the front and down the center of the room. This communicates the value and closeness the teacher has for and with each individual. Of course, some students need to sit in the corners. It's a physics problem. But we encourage you to inventory which students are seated where and to make changes regularly so that you can minimize the impact of physical and emotional distance on students' learning.

When it comes to middle and high school classrooms, Dominique likes to comment that much of the seating looks like a cemetery, with rows and columns. Given the space allocated to some learning environments, this is the only way to fit all of the students in the room. But this "cemetery seating" is not really conducive to student-to-student interaction or teacher proximity. If you are stuck with this type of seating, rotate students often, and note which students you call on. It's likely that you use the T-pattern, focused on the first two rows and the middle rows, which makes a T in your classroom (and all of the students know it). If this is happening, it needs to change.

WE ENCOURAGE YOU TO INVENTORY WHICH STUDENTS ARE SEATED WHERE AND TO MAKE CHANGES REGULARLY.

Having said that, we're not big fans of calling on students randomly. Without strong social relationships in the classroom, students feel extreme pressure and anxiety during class time. We had a candidate for a teaching position at our school engage students in a demonstration lesson. She used index cards to randomly call on students, which was not the norm in the classroom. Students were put off by this. As one of them said, after putting her head down and refusing to participate, "She doesn't know us. She can't just get up in here and call us out like that. I don't know her, and I don't trust her."

In addition, there are students who are more introverted and who need more processing time. These students may experience stress when their teachers use techniques to call on them randomly. One of our recent graduates told us about her experience as a student in elementary school, saying, "When the popsicle sticks came out, my hand would go up. I suddenly had to go to the bathroom. I wanted to avoid that. I was a good student, really good. But I'm shy, and that was terrifying."

Of course, we do see the benefits of this practice, in that it can keep students paying attention (perhaps out of fear). If you are going to use this technique, make sure that the environment is socially supportive and that students will not be humiliated by their peers for incorrect answers. As we have noted, errors should be celebrated as opportunities to learn, but that is not always the case in the classroom. There are many other ways to ensure that students engage in learning, as have been outlined in this book. Our point here is to ensure that you are physically and emotionally close to students, that they have opportunities to respond, and that you hear their responses.

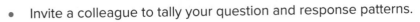

- Invite a colleague to tally your question and response patterns.
- Who did you interact with more frequently? Less frequently?
- How did these patterns intersect with the physical location of the students?
- Reflect on these questions and the data, and identify areas for change.

After you have made the changes, invite a colleague to observe again. This time, identify three students who struggle to learn in your class. Ask the observer to record the following data:

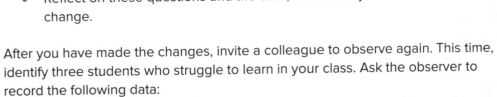

Student Name	Proximity Did the teacher stand within an arm's length of the student?	Response Opportunity Was the student provided an opportunity to respond?	Wait Time Did the teacher wait at least five seconds if the student did not respond immediately before talking?	Nonverbal Interaction Did the teacher smile, make eye contact with, or otherwise engage nonverbally with the student?

THINK ALONG

Vulnerability. Dominique discusses vulnerability. How do you demonstrate "confident vulnerability" to your students?

Others see us as available when we are vulnerable. Closeness develops when we are honest and acknowledge our weaknesses and insecurities. Having said that, you're still the teacher, and you deserve respect, but when you can make yourself vulnerable, take the opportunity. Palmer concludes that teaching is a "daily exercise in vulnerability" (1998, p. 17). As Brené Brown (2012) says,

> Vulnerability is the birthplace of love, belonging, joy, courage, empathy, and creativity. It is the source of hope, empathy, accountability, and authenticity. If we want greater clarity in our purpose or deeper and more meaningful spiritual lives, vulnerability is the path. (p. 34)

And wouldn't it be great to have all of those things in the classroom? Students are, by and large, vulnerable every day. We should be as well. Unfortunately, some people misread this as weak.

We are certainly not suggesting that teachers be weak. Instead, we hope that you engage in shared struggle and continuous exposure of the struggle. It means that you address your fears. It requires that you allow yourself to discover new things and learn new lessons. In essence, it means that you're comfortable opening up. And when you do, your immediacy with students grows. They feel closer to you and want to learn more. A few examples are worth noting.

A superintendent friend of ours was talking about his first year on the job. Overall, the teachers were intimidated by him. They respected his knowledge but were not sure of his motives. He recognized that he needed to be vulnerable to them. He engaged in a range of activities to increase his vulnerability, but one stood out to us. He decided to tell his life story to everyone. He humanized himself and gave people information about his mistakes and successes. As he said, "Someone could have used it against me, sure. But I wanted them to know me, to trust me, to see me as an ally. I had to be vulnerable to accomplish that."

Another example comes from some middle school teachers who work on a team. They regularly take the tests for classes they do not teach. They tell students in advance that they have a competition with another teacher—for example, the history teacher will compete with the math teacher—each saying that he will do better than the other on the next test. They model studying and note when they get things wrong. They share their struggles and their successes. And they share their test scores at the end. Their students love it. Not only does this open the door to additional learning, but it makes the students feel close to their teachers.

TEACHING IS A "DAILY EXERCISE IN VULNERABILITY."

More recently, there has been attention to the idea of a failure resume. For example, the *New York Times* included an article about this (Herrera, 2019), asking readers if they kept a failure resume, and suggesting why they should start one if they did not. As noted in the article, "Failure isn't a roadblock. It's part of the process."

REFLECTIVE WRITING

What would be on your failure resume?

INSIDE THE CLASSROOM

Chemistry teacher Angie Hackman took this to heart.

She knows that her subject is complex, often noted as the hardest class at her school. The students trust their teacher and her competence. She's dynamic and has a passion for her subject. And to top it all off, she is vulnerable with them. She keeps a failure resume and shares her failures with her students. A humbling example was when she did not pass the National Board Certification on her first attempt. It's now permanently part of her failure resume, and she talks about it each year with students, also noting that it eventually motivated her to try again and pass. As Mykeila said,

Ms. Hackman has had some challenges, but she doesn't let that get her down. Things didn't always work for her the first time. But she doesn't give up. And, like she says, there isn't one student name on her failure resume. She makes sure that none of us end up there. How cool is that?

Take a risk and be vulnerable with your students. Start slow, but let them see that you are a complex person who has ups and downs. Let them know you a little more so that you develop the closeness that students crave from the adults who teach them. We promise, it will pay dividends.

THE POWER OF TOUCH

We could not end this chapter without returning to the discussion of physical contact with students. We recognize that many school systems have policies that prevent any hand shaking, high fives, or the like with students.

REFLECTIVE WRITING

What is the policy on physical contact in your school system?
Is it implemented equitably?

We understand that this is an attempt to set limits and protect students. Yet we struggle with it. We are social animals, and touch conveys value and closeness. We noted the TESA work of the Los Angeles County Office of Education earlier in this chapter. One of the 15 interactions they found to accelerate the learning of students who were not achieving well was touch. Of course, there are cultural and gender boundaries, but TESA challenges assumptions about physical contact and suggests that many students respond to respectful touch. The relationships that develop when teachers can shake the hand of a student entering the room, place a hand on a student's shoulder to communicate that he or she is doing a great job, or high five a student who has completed a major project are amazing. In addition, it should be noted that teachers can "touch" with their eyes and words—the wink of an eye for a job well done, a smile at the end of the presentation, and the use of pronouns such as *we* and *our* all communicate value and respect.

ONE OF THE 15 INTERACTIONS FOUND TO ACCELERATE THE LEARNING OF STUDENTS WAS TOUCH.

But if you are not comfortable with physical contact, be consistent. In other words, if you shake hands with some students, offer to shake hands with all students. As we have noted before, students are watching, and they notice when inequitable relationships develop. Students who are not greeted with a high five notice those who are, and believe that they are less important to you.

Kindergarten teacher Amelia Huff has a sign outside her door that tells students to choose their greetings as they enter. Some choose a hug, others a high five, and still others a handshake or a wave. Each time they enter the room, they choose their greeting, whether that be first thing in the morning, after recess or lunch, or when returning from art, PE, or music. Interestingly, students change their greetings throughout the day. They are in charge, and their teacher demonstrates that they are valued and that she is close to them.

High school English teacher Antonia Reyes says,

I'm a hugger. I hug everybody. Well, if students don't want it, I don't push myself on them. But they all come to want some contact with me. I like to give a quick hug when they do amazing things, and when they return from a break or being out because they were absent. Yeah, I hug from the side, but I don't think they really notice. They just notice that I care about them and I am willing to show it.

IMMEDIACY AND COLLECTIVE EFFICACY

One element of collective efficacy that is rarely addressed is the physiological factors that contribute to or detract from the social milieu of a team. These affective factors are influenced by the same nonverbal signals discussed throughout this chapter. Eye contact, facial expression, and physical proximity contribute to a sense of closeness within the team. A team member perceived as a loner (low teacher credibility and low collective efficacy) may be signaling his emotional distance through physical remoteness, less eye contact, and fewer verbal exchanges with colleagues. Pay attention to the way the physical environment for a professional meeting is structured so that no one is disadvantaged and distanced from the conversation.

Conversely, the social structures of the team can negatively impact immediacy for students. You will recall that earlier in this chapter, second-grade teacher Patty Cole described her efforts to increase immediacy with her students during recess. Her entire team had identified immediacy as a common challenge, and they took deliberate action to disrupt the routine of clustered adults on the playground.

REFLECTIVE WRITING

Why is immediacy crucial for professional relationships? Are there patterns you've noticed in team meetings as they relate to immediacy? What might you do to shift these patterns?

"We like to talk to each other, but we asked our instructional coach to use the nonverbal immediacy scale with us," said Ms. Cole, continuing

> She helped us see that our habit of standing close together talking on the playground made it harder for students to interact with us. We decided to change our habit to increase our availability to students. Our social time is important. We also made a pact to eat lunch together three times a week, instead of giving in to the temptation to eat in our rooms and keep working. It's actually been good for all of us.

Eye contact, facial expression, and physical proximity contribute to a sense of closeness within the team.

iStock.com/SDI Productions

Improving the immediacy, or perceived closeness, of the team will likely result in improved working relationships and more productive conversations that impact students' learning. Following this chapter, we turn our attention to collective efficacy and building powerful teams that have the skills and expectations to make a difference for all students. At this point, we invite you to engage in a brief self-assessment of your team's immediacy. Identify the frequency of each of these behaviors within your team.

Our team uses appropriate levels of:

Eye contact

| Never | Sometimes | Frequently | Consistently |

Warm facial expressions

| Never | Sometimes | Frequently | Consistently |

Relaxed body positions

| Never | Sometimes | Frequently | Consistently |

Comfortable proximity

| Never | Sometimes | Frequently | Consistently |

Animated vocal expressiveness

| Never | Sometimes | Frequently | Consistently |

IMMEDIACY

PAUSE & PONDER

Now that you have analyzed the ways in which your team interacts nonverbally, consider the impact of these interaction patterns on the productivity of the team. What could you personally change? Remember, smiles are contagious. If you change some of your behaviors, the team might just adopt a different stance. When your team has significant trust, talk openly about the interaction patterns you all notice.

CONCLUDING THOUGHTS ABOUT IMMEDIACY

Immediacy is a feeling or perception. It's something that students, often unconsciously, keep track of. Their internal voice is always wondering how close they are to their teacher. Sometimes they frame this as "does my teacher like me," and they use the actions and behaviors displayed by their teacher to make a decision. Other times, they notice differential treatment as evidence of the closeness they feel toward the teacher. Regardless, we know that students' perceptions of the immediacy they have with the teacher impact their engagement, motivation, and eventually their learning. Thankfully, there are specific things we can do to increase the immediacy our students perceive, and we can slowly but surely increase the closeness they feel.

Nancy provides you with a challenge to conclude this chapter.

If you have engaged with the Pause & Ponder tasks, you've already changed your students' perceptions about their closeness to you. Now it's time to develop this with your team. Nancy's challenge is to improve the immediacy your colleagues perceive from you.

CHAPTER 5 CHALLENGE

Improve the immediacy your colleagues perceive from you.

COLLECTIVE EFFICACY
SKILLS

noun | skill | \ 'skil \

a: The ability to use one's knowledge effectively and readily in execution or performance

b: A learned power of doing something competently: a developed aptitude or ability, e.g., language *skills*

BUILDING COLLECTIVE EFFICACY

Thus far, we have focused on teacher credibility, and the bulk of the last four chapters have centered on the ways in which teacher credibility can be harnessed to improve students' learning. At the end of each chapter, we noted the impact of a specific aspect of teacher credibility on the collective efficacy of the adults. As we noted in the introduction, collective teacher efficacy refers to a staff's shared belief that through their collective action, they can positively influence student outcomes, including for students who are disengaged and/or disadvantaged. We also argued that there was a relationship between teacher credibility and collective efficacy. In general, teachers want to be around other teachers they believe are effective. Teachers hear what students have to say about their colleagues, and we all like to surround ourselves with people who we can learn from and who are as passionate and dedicated as we are.

In addition, teams need a set of skills if they are to collaborate productively. Both individual and collective skills are important. These include communication skills and relational trust. In addition, teams need supportive structures that allow them to function.

The kindergarten team at Amelia Earhart Elementary School was composed of nine teachers of varying longevity in the profession. Their personalities were different, yet they had a common mission. Some were grandmotherly, while others were more likely to run marathons or hike local mountains. Outside of work, they did not seem like they would socialize much. But at school, they were tight. They mentored new members of their team and visited each other's classrooms regularly. They shared ideas freely and debated the best ways to ensure that every student achieved. When one of the team members went on family leave, they were active in finding a long-term substitute for him. As one of them said, "We can't have just anybody. We need someone who the kids will love and someone who wants to work with us." They asked their principal if they could be part of the interview team that selected the substitute, and she agreed. This team understood that each member is important and that collectively they are powerful.

Unfortunately, as we noted in Chapter 1, there are loners out there who do not engage students in learning and who do not contribute to their teams. There are many reasons that people become loners. Some do so because they are not confident with their skill set and believe that asking for help is a sign of weakness. Others are loners because they do not trust their colleagues. There are many reasons, but regardless, they need support to change. And to our thinking, that support should come from both peers and leaders. We do not believe that school systems can fire their way to improvement, meaning that increasing student achievement is not as simple as firing people who are believed to be ineffective. Getting to the root causes that some

Introducing Collective Efficacy Skills.

LISTEN as Doug discusses the sources of collective efficacy and the need for strong communication.

team members are loners, talkers, or independent contractors can point teams in the right direction. In this chapter, we focus on the roles that peers play in creating collective efficacy. We did not say that developing collective teacher efficacy was easy, but it is powerful when it is present.

TEACHERS HEAR WHAT STUDENTS HAVE TO SAY ABOUT THEIR COLLEAGUES.

In part, we were motivated to write this book because the last decade has been difficult for teachers. Eight percent of teachers leave the teaching profession each year, and an additional 8% move to another school. A small portion of these changes are due to retirement. The Learning Policy Institute (LPI) estimates that 67% of all teacher turnovers each year are due to people leaving for reasons other than retirement (Carver-Thomas & Darling-Hammond, 2017). More recently, LPI reported that in 2018, 7.3% of then-practicing teachers were planning to leave. (See an interactive state-by-state map at https://learningpolicyinstitute.org/product/understanding-teacher-shortages-interactive.) The reasons for leaving or moving are revealing. Compensation is relatively low on the list; collegiality in the school is often cited as an important factor weighing on their decision to leave or stay. Principal turnover data are even more dire, with 18–21% of principals leaving their position each year (Levin & Bradley, 2019). The factor exiting teachers and principals cite as a common reason for leaving? The quality of collegial relationships.

The churn created by teacher and principal turnover creates a strain on the teachers who remain, the students at the school, and their families. In addition, it further erodes the relational conditions that bind educators and leaders to school organizations. Schools with high turnover experience a downward spiral in morale and in their collective efficacy. The revolving door serves as a disincentive to invest in one another as professionals and as colleagues. A bunker mentality grows as individuals hunker down to do their own thing, and the result is social disorganization. In neighborhoods, social disorganization is associated with higher crime rates. In schools, it is associated with lower collective teacher efficacy.

NOTES

Using the "traffic light" scale, identify your strengths as a team. As you think about each of these dimensions, ask yourself "Does our team . . ."

1. Trust one another?

2. Exhibit caring relationships for one another?

3. Give and accept feedback from one another?

4. Celebrate individual and group successes?

5. Know how to mediate each other's thinking?

6. Resolve conflict and make decisions?

SKILLS

PAUSE & PONDER

What do you notice about your team? What changes could you make to improve the productivity of the team?

SUPPORTIVE STRUCTURES FOR BUILDING COLLECTIVE EFFICACY

You will recall from previous chapters that a group's collective efficacy draws from four sources: mastery experiences, vicarious experiences, social persuasion, and affective and physiological factors (Bandura, 1997). As a reminder, mastery experiences relate to firsthand success, while vicarious experiences are the successes of others with whom we share an affinity. The third source of collective efficacy is our ability to persuade each other due to our credibility and trustworthiness. The fourth source draws from our dispositions and mood, as well as our biological state. Each of these is directly impacted by our relationships with one another. Relationships are the glue that holds us together.

The social cohesion of an organization should not be confused with friendships. These are personal in nature, and while some friendships may emerge in the workplace, they are not necessary. Indeed, many of us can name friends we couldn't work with very effectively. The social cohesion of an organization is the "willingness of its members to cooperate" with one another (Stanley, 2003, p. 6). That said, we must create supportive relational conditions that contribute to social cohesion. These include supportive structures and communication tools.

Time is a barrier to building productive relationships with colleagues. We spend the majority of our working hours in the company of students. The relative number of adults we interact with is small compared to the number of staff. In addition, these exchanges are typically either social or transactional in nature. Pleasantries are shared, and we're able to obtain an extra ream of copy paper, but there's no time for discussion of practice.

An additional barrier is that we rarely get to see what others are doing. This can breed a sense of isolation and introduce doubt about whether colleagues are similarly engaged in agreed efforts. Doug and Nancy saw this take root years ago when they worked at a high school that had agreed to daily independent reading. The schedule had been redesigned to accommodate the 20-minute period without loss of instructional minutes to the second-period classes in which it was supposed to occur. Yet despite professional development and purchase of reading materials, the uptake was far less than expected. Private conversations with teachers revealed what was going on. As many explained, it wasn't that they didn't think a dedicated independent reading period was worthwhile. Rather, they questioned whether they were the only ones doing it.

"I don't want to stop my instruction to do this," explained one teacher, "if I'm the only one doing it. Why bother if no one else cares?"

Our solution was a monthly two-minute video shown at each professional development meeting.

> WE MUST CREATE SUPPORTIVE RELATIONAL CONDITIONS THAT CONTRIBUTE TO SOCIAL COHESION.

REFLECTIVE WRITING

How might an opportunity to see your colleagues in action change your practices?

_____

_____

_____

_____

_____

_____

_____

_____

_____

_____

_____

_____

_____

_____

_____

The content always focused on an aspect of independent reading, but the covert message was conveyed through the visuals. Each video featured a multitude of teachers and students across campus reading independently during this time. In a short while, nearly all the teachers were full participants in the program. The only thing that changed was that they got to witness their colleagues' shared efforts.

Hord (1997) who coined the term _professional learning communities,_ identified organizational structures as one of two critical conditions for promoting school improvement efforts. (The other is collegial relationships.) Teachers need time and communication procedures in order to engage in meaningful ways. Time to meet with colleagues is part of every bargaining contract and can include grade or department meetings, PLCs, instructional leadership teams, impact teams, and the like. At the school where the three of us work, we augmented weekly meetings with a daily routine to continually invest in the social cohesion of the staff. Our morning meeting is a ten-minute daily standing meeting for every adult at the school and is held at the beginning of the contract day. Classified and certificated staff stands in a circle in a large classroom, while a rotating cadre of school leaders facilitates the meeting. There are three agenda items:

1. **"What do we need to know for today to be successful?"**

   Current information about events: This may cover field trips, testing schedules, and other time-sensitive information.

2. **A spotlight on students and colleagues for recognition or of concern**

This is really the centerpiece of morning meeting, as colleagues discuss concerns about students. This is crucial, as staff members recognize that many people have relationships with the student and can be of assistance. Problems aren't solved in the morning meeting; plans are rapidly put in place to meet right after it or later in the day to address next steps. This strikes directly at the heart of collective efficacy: the "aggregate capacity of a community to work toward common goals" (Reid & Pell, 2015, p. 322).

3. **An ongoing culture-building activity**

The third routine is meant to focus on the collective commitment we have to one another's well-being. At the end of each meeting, one staff member shares a personal comment that is based on a prompt based on an area of common focus. This comment closes the meeting, and the person speaking identifies the person who will share the following day. For example, we might be focused on examples of teamwork or demonstrated commitment to students or our personal journey at the school. Typically, there is a physical item that serves as the talking piece. Over the years we have signed t-shirts, basketballs, and large framed photographs, written journal entries, and inserted wishes into a giant metal fortune cookie. Each area of focus takes about two months, so that each member of the staff has a chance to contribute to that focus. The result is that we learn more about one another. And by the way, we eliminated weekly after-school staff meetings.

THINK ALONG

Morning Meeting.
Dominique shares what one school does to ensure that teachers connect with each other daily. Do you have a regularly scheduled time for staff to connect? What are your hunches about what this might accomplish at your school?

The cumulative 50 minutes a week we spend together in the morning means that we have a forum to exchange information. Psychologically, the effect is that we recommit to one another each day. The lingering conversations after the meeting, before adults walk to their classrooms and desks, suggests that the social network is continually strengthened and expanded.

NOTES

COMMUNICATION TOOLS BUILD COLLECTIVE EFFICACY

It is tempting to fall into the trap of assuming that adults know how to work together in growth-producing ways. However, experience suggests otherwise. Many of the formally structured interactions mandated by the school (e.g., grade or department meetings, professional learning communities) result in what Newberry, Sanchez, and Clark (2018) call contrived relationships. These meetings have an "administrative focus [but] lack the emotional depth that teachers need to support the emotion work they perform daily" (p. 33). They note that without attention to the emotional subtext of these interactions, deeper working relationships are inhibited due to differing practices and philosophies. Members are therefore reluctant to share ideas or beliefs, as they have been reinforced to "relate to one another as 'educators' rather than fellow human beings" (Shapiro, 2007, p. 618).

In order to deepen the social cohesion of the group, members need to utilize communication tools that signal active listening and the supportive exchanges of ideas. The seven norms of collaborative work from cognitive coaching are useful for developing communication skills that address the relational elements essential to deep collaboration (Costa & Garmston, 2015).

THE SEVEN NORMS OF COLLABORATIVE WORK

1. Pausing
2. Paraphrasing
3. Posing questions
4. Providing data
5. Putting ideas on the table
6. Paying attention to self and others
7. Presuming positive intentions

SKILLS

INSIDE THE CLASSROOM

This video focuses on wait time. What benefits have you seen in using wait time with students? With adults?

PAUSING

Deceptively simple, pausing provides opportunities for speakers to extend their thinking and for listeners to consider what has been said. The opposite of speaking is not waiting to speak again; it's listening. Pausing is analogous to the wait time practices we know are critical to foster student discourse. Wait time is used in classrooms because it has been reliably shown to encourage longer student responses and more critical thinking (Tobin, 1987). Purposeful pausing allows time for the listeners to process what has been said before attempting to share additional information. Pausing gives the speaker time to consider her own ideas. It also signals to the speakers and the listeners that contributions are valued.

Pausing provides opportunities for speakers to extend their thinking and for listeners to consider what has been said.

iStock.com/SDI Productions

SKILLS

PAUSE & PONDER

	I never do this.	I rarely do this.	I sometimes do this.	I consistently do this.
Refrain from speaking over others				
Allow time when the speaker finishes before adding information				
Actively listen when others are speaking				

My goal for using pausing in professional conversations is . . .

_____

_____

_____

_____

_____

_____

_____

_____

_____

_____

_____

_____

_____

_____

_____

_____

PARAPHRASING

Costa and Garmston (2015) note that paraphrasing is an underutilized communication tool. Yet paraphrasing has the potential to move the group's thinking forward. The speaker's statements are recast to ensure that what has been understood is accurate and complete. However, there is an intentional avoidance of "I-statements," as they can shift the attention from the speaker to the person paraphrasing. Note that in the examples below, I-statements are not used. The authors suggest that there are three ways to paraphrase:

1. **Use acknowledging statements,** for example,

   "You're concerned about . . ."

   "You're wondering if . . ."

2. **Organize the member's statement**, for example,

   "So, there are four things you're concerned about."

   "On the one hand _____, and on the other hand _____."

   This paraphrasing technique is especially useful when speakers are recounting experiences that they have not yet fully processed.

3. **Attempt to elevate the speaker's thinking from an anecdote to a larger but perhaps unstated issue**; this is called *abstraction*. For example,

   "So, a goal of yours is . . ."

   "You value . . ."

   Paraphrasing confers the group's respect and confirms the value of the speaker, who hears the emotional subtext: "We are striving to understand you."

PAUSE & PONDER

	I never do this.	I rarely do this.	I sometimes do this.	I consistently do this.
I acknowledge the ideas of others.				
I help organize the thinking of others.				
I attempt to link speakers' ideas to larger issues.				
I avoid using I-statements when paraphrasing.				

My goal for using paraphrasing in professional conversations is . . .

POSING QUESTIONS

Once an initial understanding has been reached, the group can pose questions. The first are those that further clarify the details, are factual in nature, and are closed types of questions, for example,

"How many students were in the group?"

Once necessary details have been covered, open-ended probes should be utilized.

REFLECTIVE WRITING

How might these communication tools, based on cognitive coaching, help you and your team work more effectively?

Costa and Garmston (2015) caution that these are not thinly veiled suggestions (e.g., "Have you ever considered using a graphic organizer?"). Rather, the intention is to mediate the speaker's thinking. One of our favorites from the cognitive coaching framework is to ask, "What are your hunches about _____?" and then let the person talk.

You'll know that your probing questions are doing the job when you hear speakers respond with their own reflective insights. Taken together, pausing, paraphrasing, and posing questions compose a cycle of norms put into action. Far more than the norm, "listen as an ally, these three techniques convey that members are valued, listened to without judgment, and seen as people, not just as educators. Think about how valued you would feel if your team utilized these three techniques. But there are even more techniques that teams can use.

You'll know that your probing questions are doing the job when you hear speakers respond with their own reflective insights.

iStock.com/SDI Productions

PAUSE & PONDER

	I never do this.	I rarely do this.	I sometimes do this.	I consistently do this.
Clarifying factual questions are asked when additional details are needed.				
Open-ended probes are used to mediate the speakers' thinking.				
Questions elicit additional ideas and information from the speaker.				

My goal for posing questions in professional conversations is . . .

PROVIDING DATA

The experiences of members are crucial for teams to identify their collective work. These experiences should be mirrored in the qualitative and quantitative data available to the team. We suspect that whenever we mention data, most immediately think of state test scores. These are not unimportant, but we do believe they have cast a long shadow over the data that are right in front of us. Exit slips, student questions, an email from a parent, the results of last night's homework—all of these are data sources. We will discuss data sources in more detail in the next chapter. In the context of communication, how we discuss the data can pose a barrier for teams.

There are three elements that are essential to data discussion. The first is to depersonalize the data. Rather than frame it as "*your* third-period results" or "*our* intervention program," try using depersonalized language: "the results" or "the program." It's human nature to feel defensive when data you are involved with are negative. Nonjudgmental and depersonalized data discussions build a sense of safety and trust in the group. The second element in a data discussion is striving to find the story behind the data. This is especially important when the data are quantitative, as the numbers can eclipse the humans they represent and the context in which they were gathered. The third element of data collection is asking what other data might broaden the group's understanding. Be careful that the data are not explained away. It takes courage to stick with the data and act upon them. The team's willingness to sit with the data, consider possibilities, and seek to understand the underlying story signal a caring but resolute disposition.

Exit slips, student questions, an email from a parent, the results of last night's homework—all of these are data sources.

iStock.com/PeopleImages

PAUSE & PONDER

	I never do this.	I rarely do this.	I sometimes do this.	I consistently do this.
Conversations about data are neutral.				
The contexts of data are discussed.				
Discussions remained focused on data.				

My goal for providing data in professional conversations is . . .

_____

_____

_____

_____

_____

_____

_____

_____

_____

_____

_____

_____

_____

_____

_____

_____

_____

_____

_____

_____

SKILLS

PUTTING IDEAS ON THE TABLE

Collective efficacy will not develop if the group does not take action. However, exchanges of ideas are often filtered through the relationships that we have with individual members. Therefore, we often speak about feelings rather than the ideas themselves (Costa & Garmston, 2015). You might find that to be a surprising statement in a chapter about relational conditions, but hear us out. If the person who suggests an idea is in a particular role or is a knowledge authority, the group may be reluctant to challenge the idea because of the source (even when it's a dumb idea). Two members who have a history of conflict between them may not be able to entertain the possibility that the other person's idea was a good one. Two members who are friends agree with each other no matter what, because they don't want to risk hurt feelings. A member's ideas are disregarded because he has the least credibility with his students. In fact, this is the stage when the wheels can come off the proverbial bus. The team finds itself unable to move forward, or moves in the wrong direction, because the relationships got in the way.

COLLECTIVE EFFICACY WILL NOT DEVELOP IF THE GROUP DOES NOT TAKE ACTION.

Putting ideas on the table and considering their merit is characteristic of high-performing groups (Senge et al., 2012). In order to interrogate ideas without masking them, use neutral language to separate the idea from the person. For instance, a person who has a role of knowledge authority can preface statements by saying, "I'm not advocating for this idea. I'm thinking aloud about . . ." Here are other suggestions for forwarding ideas in a neutral way:

"A possible idea would be . . ."

"Would you consider . . .?"

"What if . . .?"

It's just as important to take ideas *off* the table (Costa & Garmston, 2015). When the discussion seems to get stuck in the proverbial cul-de-sac of circular thinking, you can say, "It seems like this idea is blocking our thinking. Let's set it aside for now and come back to it again later if we still think it's relevant."

REFLECTIVE WRITING

Have you ever taken something off the table, or have you only been to meetings where things are added to the table?

None of us have extra time, so consider what you can take off the table.

Another technique is to lasso ideas, posing further questions to clarify the group's thinking. Asking, for instance, "What do we all think we mean when we say . . . ?" can aid the group in looking again at what might be vague terminology. For instance, it is one thing to say that the group wants to develop students' skills for engaging in collaborative discussion. But it is also worthwhile to ensure that there is agreement about what constitutes discussion.

The final two norms encompass the habits and dispositions of the team as it relates to the affective and physiological aspects of collective efficacy. Our mood can bias how we perceive, attend to, interpret, and cognitively organize the ideas being discussed (Bandura, 1997). The intent isn't to remove these mood states—that would be impossible. As humans we continually process the world through our own specific emotional states. But emotional states are not necessarily the same for everyone in the room. Therefore, it is wise to attend to our own emotions and the signals others use to let us know what theirs are.

PAUSE & PONDER

	I never do this.	I rarely do this.	I sometimes do this.	I consistently do this.
Use neutral language to separate ideas from people				
Offer ideas to the group for consideration				
Focus on the ideas on the table rather than who suggested the idea				
Recognize when ideas need to be taken off the table				

My goal for putting ideas on the table in professional conversations is . . .

PAY ATTENTION TO SELF AND OTHERS

Social sensitivity is the ability to perceive and understand the feelings of others. *Social cohesion*—the glue that binds us together—is a product in part of the social sensitivity of the members of a group or organization. Be mindful not only of what you say, but how the message appears to be received by others. Their posture, facial expressions, position, movement, gestures, and eye contact speak volumes that convey far more information than words alone. It is useful to maintain curiosity about the emotional states of others while resisting the urge to react defensively. "I felt a shift in the mood when I proposed that idea," you might say. "Help me understand the reaction."

Your own mood is also important. Take an inventory of your impressions as you consider ideas. Did you notice yourself tense up when a particular suggestion was made by another member? If so, don't judge yourself, but instead ask yourself what might be lurking behind the reaction. Perhaps a previous experience did not go well for you, and now you are struggling to reconcile the past with a possible future action. If you need to, ask the group to help you process the experience in order to understand it better. The first three communication tools—pause, paraphrase, and pose questions—will assist you and the team with working through what might otherwise be an obstacle to action.

It is useful to maintain curiosity about the emotional states of others while resisting the urge to react defensively.
iStock.com/kali9

PAUSE & PONDER

	I never do this.	I rarely do this.	I sometimes do this.	I consistently do this.
Monitor personal reactions to ideas and people				
Monitor nonverbal behaviors to foster social cohesion				
Notice the behaviors and actions of others to gain understanding of their mood				

My goal for paying attention to myself and others in professional conversations is . . .

_____

_____

_____

_____

_____

_____

_____

_____

_____

_____

_____

_____

_____

_____

_____

PRESUME POSITIVE INTENTIONS

This could be first, last, and everything in between. It is a tool and also a disposition and requires action in order to sustain it. Too often, this norm appears on the list for a group at the beginning of the school year and is then quickly forgotten. While open confrontation is rare, the more common response is that members refrain from sharing ideas, thus stunting the agency of the group. Please recognize that your colleagues are doing the best they know how, as are you. It is rare that any educator wakes up in the morning and thinks, "I choose to ruin Dave's day today." (By the way, students don't do this, either.) And yet it happens. Recognize that there are times when we mar someone else's day.

Reframe statements such that they convey a presumption of positive intentions. Saying, "Our writing scores went down despite our efforts last quarter. What's wrong?" puts everyone on the defensive, and the blame game begins. In an attempt to deflect, we blame the assessment, the curriculum, the students, the two snow days we had last month . . . anything to redirect it away from ourselves. In an attempt to maintain the social cohesion, there might be a member who takes the hit for the team. "I didn't do a good job. That's probably why the scores went down." Mind you, there are no data to support that statement, just a desperate need to break the tension. A reframed statement might be,

> "We've got a shared commitment to increasing our students' writing skills. There's lots of things we did last quarter to do so. But the data suggest that we didn't accomplish what we intended. Let's take a closer look at what we think might be contributing to the gap between what we want and where we're at right now."

The reframed statement takes more words, but it is what the emotional brain hears that is crucial. There is an acknowledgment to a shared commitment and to effort, both of which presume positive intention. There is also acknowledgment of a gap that persists. The team is undaunted by the gap. They draw on their collective efficacy as a source of strength.

The undercurrent of exchanges such as this is the relational trust the members share. The elements of relational trust directly contribute to the social cohesion of the group, as peers support peers in meaningful ways.

Importantly, we are not only referring to the procedures for peer support, such as learning walks and such. At the heart of relational trust is how we are able to draw on each other in challenging situations.

SKILLS

INSIDE THE CLASSROOM

Watch an elementary team work together to craft success criteria. How many of the communication tools are they using to foster their collective efficacy?

	I never do this.	I rarely do this.	I sometimes do this.	I consistently do this.
Reframe statements such that they convey a presumption of positive intentions				
Revisit group norms				
Work to maintain and enhance relational trust				

My goal for presuming positive intentions in professional conversations is . . .

_____

_____

_____

_____

_____

_____

_____

_____

_____

_____

_____

_____

_____

_____

_____

SKILLS

COLLECTIVE EFFICACY AND RELATIONAL TRUST

In response to a 2010 court order, the Los Angeles Unified School District (LAUSD) approached a team of researchers to help them answer questions about persistent teacher turnover in 45 of the district's most challenging schools. These schools were perpetually destabilized as teachers and leaders came and went. The district concentrated significant resources in these schools to improve conditions, including salary incentives, professional learning, and investment in organizational structures. These organizational structure improvements focused on the development of social cohesion and trust among teachers and leaders. But the district wondered: "Should district interventions be aimed at schoolwide improvements or individually focused incentives?" (Fuller, Waite, & Irribarra, 2016, p. 547).

The answer proved to be a complex one and did not yield a yes to one alternative and a no to the other. However, it is important to say that while incentives were a factor, they were not overwhelmingly so. Relationships mattered to the 548 teachers in this study. "How teachers view coherent features of their schools—the leadership team, trusting relations among colleagues, and pulling together to lift achievement—was more strongly associated with the desire to stay at or leave these challenging schools" (p. 561). Teachers who chose to stay, as well as those who chose to leave, valued the social organization of the school and described those factors as being intrinsically motivating.

There's that word again: *trust*. Just as it plays a determining role in perceptions of teacher credibility with students, it is an equally important factor in the relational conditions that contribute to collective efficacy. Trust among colleagues has been shown to be a crucial condition for productive working relationships across 20 years of work in Chicago Public Schools (Bryk, Sebring, Allensworth, Luppescu, & Easton, 2010) and is a reliable determinant of who will stay and who will leave the schools in that district (Allensworth, Ponisciak, & Mazzeo, 2009).

We have referred to teacher turnover several times in this chapter, and while it is a significant problem, we see it as the tip of the iceberg. For every teacher who chooses to leave the school or the profession, there are an unknown number of other teachers who can't or won't leave. Instead, they retreat. They close their classroom doors and keep their practice private. When they struggle, they do so alone. When they experience success they celebrate, but there is no spread of effect. Knowing what works is crucial in school improvement efforts. Without trust, we have silos of excellence and silos of suffering. Neither condition benefits students or the schools they attend.

Trust, as you will recall from Chapter 2, occurs when two people mutually believe that the other is benevolent, reliable, competent, honest, and open (Hoy & Tschannen-Moran, 2003).

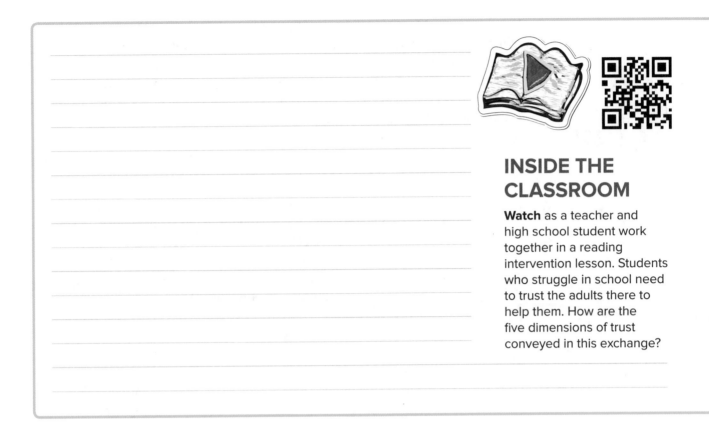

INSIDE THE CLASSROOM

Watch as a teacher and high school student work together in a reading intervention lesson. Students who struggle in school need to trust the adults there to help them. How are the five dimensions of trust conveyed in this exchange?

This is sometimes referred to as relational trust and was reported in the longitudinal Chicago school studies as being a critical ingredient for those schools that enjoyed sustained improvement (Bryk & Schneider, 2003). Relational trust among adults, according to the authors, arises as a result of the following:

- Mutual respect
- Personal regard
- Competence in core responsibilities
- Personal integrity

The seven norms of communication we just discussed are tools designed to contribute to a growing sense of trust among a group of adults. Now let's look at the four qualities that build relational trust.

Mutual respect is foundational to the work that we do. As adults we generally know how to have respectful interactions with others. In the context of collective efficacy, respect underpins our exchanges as we disagree with one another. When respect is lost due to rude or hurtful statements, some participants withdraw to avoid a demeaning situation. Others may lash out and make the situation even worse. Communication tools such as putting ideas on the table and examining data help to guide interactions that might otherwise be tense. Above all, the presumption of good intentions can save a team from damaging their collective efficacy.

SKILLS

Personal regard for one another is a further expression of the social cohesion of the group. Personal regard goes beyond the professional expectations of working interactions. Openness, sharing personal stories, laughing about a funny student remark—these are ways in which we show our personal regard for others. Dominique asks all of us to do a brief emotional check-in with one another at the start of our weekly professional learning sessions. As one memorable example, we were asked to match each staff member to his or her first car. Who knew that one of our millennial colleagues had a 1968 Volkswagen bus that he dubbed the Mystery Machine in honor of Scooby Doo?

WHEN SCHOOL LEADERS FAIL TO ADDRESS PERSISTENT INCOMPETENCE, DISTRUST SPREADS ACROSS THE ORGANIZATION.

Competence in core responsibilities is another quality that crosses over to teacher credibility. Each member of the school community has specific role responsibilities, and all are in turn dependent on one another's competent execution of those duties. Teams of teachers charged with accelerating student learning are likewise dependent on one another to enact the agreed-upon plan. The calculus of judging the competence of others includes assessments of their skill and effort. When either or both are in question and are part of a larger pattern of incompetence, teachers look internally to their own team and outwardly to school leaders. When school leaders fail to address persistent incompetence, distrust spreads across the organization. Teacher distrust at the organizational level is a significant barrier to school improvement (Bryk & Schneider, 2003) and collective teacher efficacy (Goddard, Goddard, Kim, & Miller, 2015).

Personal integrity is the final component of relational trust and is a function of a person's honesty and reliability. This is the fundamental measure of how we determine whether a person deserves our trust. In the educational setting, one's personal integrity is further judged on "commitment to the education and welfare of children" (Bryk & Schneider, 2003, p. 42).

The personal integrity of the team is compromised when they choose to ignore the incompetence and lack of credibility of a colleague. Covering for a colleague who is doing educational harm to students weakens the relational trust among the group. Failing to extend support to a struggling colleague telegraphs a signal to others that each member is on his or her own when it is difficult. Little wonder that the teachers interviewed in challenging LAUSD schools placed such importance on relational trust as a reason to stay or leave. High-functioning teams trust one another to take action when educational harm is done, or when a member is grappling with a difficult situation.

INSIDE THE CLASSROOM

Observe a high school history team as they work together with the English learner coordinator. How are the four qualities of relational trust expressed?

A MEASURE OF FACULTY TRUST

In this chapter, we have primarily addressed trust of colleagues, as it is a crucial component of collective teacher efficacy. Having said that, we need to acknowledge that trust extends in three directions:

- Trust of colleagues
- Trust of school leaders
- Trust of students

Hoy and Tschannen-Moran (2003) developed and validated a scale of faculty trust across these three dimensions. Their work on the faculty trust scales inspired the efforts of Adams and Forsyth (2009) to develop the Student Trust in Faculty Scale featured in Chapter 2. The Faculty Trust in Schools Scale is represented by the scale in Figure 6.1. The scoring key for each of the three dimensions is as follows:

- Faculty trust in the principal—sum the values for items 1, 4*, 7, 9, 11*, 15, 18, 23*
- Faculty trust in colleagues—sum the values for items 2, 5, 8*, 12, 13, 16, 19, 21
- Faculty trust in the clients—sum the values for items 3, 6, 10, 14, 17, 20, 22, 24, 25, 26*

    *Items are reverse scored; that is, [1 = 6, 2 = 5, 3 = 4, 4 = 3, 5 = 2, 6 = 1]

Further direction for obtaining standard scores is available at www.waynekhoy .com/faculty-trust/.

Figure 6.1 The Faculty Trust in Schools Scale

Directions: Please indicate your level of agreement with each of the following statements about your school from **Strongly Disagree** to **Strongly Agree**. Your answers are confidential.

	Strongly Disagree	Disagree	Somewhat Disagree	Somewhat Agree	Agree	Strongly Agree
1. Teachers in this school trust the principal.	①	②	③	④	⑤	⑥
2. Teachers in this school trust each other.	①	②	③	④	⑤	⑥
3. Teachers in this school trust their students.	①	②	③	④	⑤	⑥
4. The teachers in this school are suspicious of most of the principal's actions.	①	②	③	④	⑤	⑥
5. Teachers in this school typically look out for each other.	①	②	③	④	⑤	⑥
6. Teachers in this school trust the parents.	①	②	③	④	⑤	⑥
7. The teachers in this school have faith in the integrity of the principal.	①	②	③	④	⑤	⑥
8. Teachers in this school are suspicious of each other.	①	②	③	④	⑤	⑥
9. The principal in this school typically acts in the best interests of teachers.	①	②	③	④	⑤	⑥
10. Students in this school care about each other.	①	②	③	④	⑤	⑥
11. The principal of this school does not show concern for the teachers.	①	②	③	④	⑤	⑥
12. Even in difficult situations, teachers in this school can depend on each other.	①	②	③	④	⑤	⑥
13. Teachers in this school do their jobs well.	①	②	③	④	⑤	⑥
14. Parents in this school are reliable in their commitments.	①	②	③	④	⑤	⑥
15. Teachers in this school can rely on the principal.	①	②	③	④	⑤	⑥

(Continued)

Figure 6.1 (Continued)

	Strongly Disagree	Disagree	Somewhat Disagree	Somewhat Agree	Agree	Strongly Agree
16. Teachers in this school have faith in the integrity of their colleagues.	①	②	③	④	⑤	⑥
17. Students in this school can be counted on to do their work.	①	②	③	④	⑤	⑥
18. The principal in this school is competent in doing his or her job.	①	②	③	④	⑤	⑥
19. The teachers in this school are open with each other.	①	②	③	④	⑤	⑥
20. Teachers can count on parental support.	①	②	③	④	⑤	⑥
21. When teachers in this school tell you something, you can believe it.	①	②	③	④	⑤	⑥
22. Teachers here believe students are competent learners.	①	②	③	④	⑤	⑥
23. The principal doesn't tell teachers what is really going on.	①	②	③	④	⑤	⑥
24. Teachers think that most of the parents do a good job.	①	②	③	④	⑤	⑥
25. Teachers can believe what parents tell them.	①	②	③	④	⑤	⑥
26. Students here are secretive.	①	②	③	④	⑤	⑥

Hoy, W.K., & Tscannen-Moran, M. (2003). The conceptualization and measurement of faculty trust in schools: The omnibus T-Scale. In W.K. Hoy and C.G. Miskel (Eds.), *Studies in leading and organizing schools* (181–208). Greenwich, CT: Information Age Publishing.

Work with your leadership team to administer and analyze the results of this survey. Use the following protocol to link your decisions to your goal of building collective efficacy. First record your own thoughts and then collaborate with your team members to discuss the thoughts of the group.

Question	My Thoughts	Our Collective Thoughts
In what ways has the data collection and analysis process impacted us?		
Do we feel confident that we can meet the needs of our students?		
How will we support the decisions our team has made?		
How might the common challenge change our collective work?		

SKILLS

WHEN TRUST IS BROKEN

Before we are educators, we are humans, and as such we are flawed individuals. Schools are complex organizations held together by a complex network of relationships. However, the relational trust that is the engine that drives the collective mission of a school is fragile and at times must be repaired. Harsh words, gossip, and broken promises damage the social cohesion of teams. Without tools to repair these relationships, teams can find themselves perpetuating a cycle of dysfunction that chips away at their collective efficacy. The insidious nature of these seemingly small betrayals can become a part of the group's identity. Many of us can readily point to a grade level or department that had a reputation of distrust. These are open secrets and damage the credibility of the team in the eyes of others. "Never mind what the third-grade team says," you might think to yourself. "They can't even get their own house in order."

Broken trust is challenging to repair, and for that reason alone many shy away from even attempting to do so. But the consequences of letting it fester are too significant. Reina and Reina (2010) have researched broken trust in the workplace and have developed a seven-step plan for rebuilding trust.

THINK ALONG

Repairing Trust. Dominique discusses ways to rebuild trust. Have you tried any of these strategies? Are there relationships at school that need to be rebuilt? Can you use any of these tools to do so?

It is important to note that rebuilding trust is not a single event, but rather a process that unspools over time. A clear path for how to rebuild trust is a critical tool for teams and leaders. There are several ways that trust can be rebuilt, including the following:

1. **Observe and acknowledge what has happened.** Broken trust is understood as a loss to those involved, and therefore the first step is to name what has been lost (Reina & Reina, 2010). It is essential to mourn what could have been, and to listen carefully to those who have experienced it as a violation. This should be done face to face, as the nuances of communication, especially the nonverbal signals, are lost in emails.

2. **Allow feelings to surface.** Team meetings and one-to-one conversations can provide a forum for those who have experienced the loss of trust to work through their feelings. These should be conducted in a safe environment, perhaps with a facilitator who can aid in the communication. Emotionally safe settings are essential and prevent people's true feelings from going underground, where they can fester (Reina & Reina, 2010).

3. **Get and give support.** Depending on the nature of the broken trust, those who are on both sides of the problem need support to move forward. Those who have experienced broken trust can get stuck. A neutral facilitator, a counselor, or another colleague can be useful resources. The person who has violated the trust may also get stuck and have difficulty in being able to accept the emotional responses of the team. The employee assistance program is a more formal tool and can be a lifeline. One element of support that is often overlooked, the authors note, is the importance of information. Broken trust often sparks a feeling of having been blindsided. Information that is accurate and current restores confidence and a feeling of being "in the know." If you have been the person who has broken trust with others, keep them informed of what you are doing to rebuild their faith in you.

4. **Reframe the experience.** This step is not about providing a justification but rather identifying the lessons learned. "Acknowledging what you have learned through a situation, as painful as the situation may be," write the authors, "supports healing" (p. 70). This is true for the person who has violated trust as well as those who have suffered from it. There are choices and opportunities moving forward, but these will not be apparent if there is no attempt to unearth them.

5. **Take responsibility.** This is truth telling, and it is something all parties participate in. For the person who has violated the trust, it is an apology that is unblemished by excuses, justifications, or rationalizations. For those who have been the victims, it is taking responsibility for their reactions, and in some cases their enabling contributions to the development of the situation. This is also a time for taking action to move forward. When trust is broken, those who have been the victims of the breakdown need to name what actions are needed. Unless they do so, the group becomes stuck and cannot move forward. Reina and Reina suggest these questions for determining action (p. 84):

   - Which of my needs still need to be addressed?
   - What problem do I need to solve?

- What information do I need, and where can I get it?

- What actions can I take now to take charge of the situation?

- What conversations do I need to have?

- What do I need to set straight?

6. **Forgive yourself and others.** It is common for those who have been the victim of a betrayal to ruminate on the signs they missed. "How did I not see this coming?" they ask. The damaging effect of continued self-recrimination is that the hope of rebuilding trust is closed off. Keep in mind that the collective efficacy of the group, and the credibility of individuals, thrives on trust. Self-forgiveness is a necessary part of the process of rebuilding trust. Forgiveness of self shines a light on the path to forgiving others.

7. **Let go and move on.** Hanging on to past injustices is corrosive for those who have experienced broken trust; remembering is not. Trust is not rebuilt in a single day, and it would be foolish to advise people to simply forget about what has occurred. But moving forward should always be a goal for rebuilding trust. Teams have a shared responsibility in doing so.

We rarely see issues of trust and its breakdown addressed in anything written for teachers.

REFLECTIVE WRITING

The process for repairing trust is emotional yet powerful. With whom do you need to repair trust, and how will you start?

It seems to be assumed that adults know how to do these things. Yet experience and observation suggest otherwise. Social cohesion and relational trust are essential dimensions of credibility and collective efficacy. But they are also incredibly fragile. If we don't have the tools and the emotional space to address this issue, we risk our capacity to fulfill our mission: to attend to the education and welfare of the students we serve.

CONCLUDING THOUGHTS ABOUT COLLECTIVE EFFICACY SKILLS

We draw our collective strength from the social cohesion and relational trust we build with our colleagues. The agendas, goal-setting protocols, written plans, and data analysis tools are all for naught if we are unable to draw on this as a source of strength. Our collective efficacy is bound up in our beliefs about the benevolence, reliability, competence, honesty, and openness of the adults we work most closely with each day. And when we have strong communication skills, real work gets done, and teams experience mastery and are much more likely to continue their work. Of course, impact is the fodder of collective efficacy. When teams realize results, and take some time to recognize and celebrate their successes, collective efficacy is strengthened.

Nancy provides you with a challenge to conclude this chapter. In this case, she asks you to adopt some of the communication tools outlined in this chapter. Pick something that is hard for you. Perhaps you are not used to pausing to allow others to complete their thoughts. Or perhaps you forget to pose questions. Try on these tools, and monitor the ways in which your team responds.

CHAPTER 6 CHALLENGE

Adopt some of the communication tools outlined in this chapter.

COLLECTIVE EFFICACY IN
ACTION

noun | ac·tion | \ˈak-shən\

a: A thing done: deed

b: The accomplishment of a thing usually over a period of time, in stages, or with the possibility of repetition

COLLECTIVE EFFORT AND COLLABORATION

"We've got our work cut out for us. I'm glad I'm not doing this alone."

James McIntyre, the math department chair at his middle school, was speaking about the changes they were experiencing. Their district had rolled out new eighth-grade algebra-for-all requirements for the following school year that would be challenging to meet. In addition, the long-time principal at their building had been promoted to a district position and had taken several key personnel with her.

Not all of the math faculty members were sold on the idea of algebra course work in eighth grade, either. Some discussed the mixed findings regarding policy and practice and its impact on equity initiatives (e.g., Remillard, Baker, Steele, Hoe, & Traynor, 2017). However, the team was solid in two areas: (1) belief in their students and (2) belief in each other as members of a team. And although the leadership structure at the school was currently in flux, they had developed a cohesive culture as a school. Three years ago, the now-departed principal had restructured planning time so that teachers worked within two professional learning communities—in content area groups and within their assigned grade levels. The result was that these teachers had far more knowledge of the credibility of colleagues teaching the other core subjects. As a math department, they enacted several processes designed to promote their knowledge of one another as teachers, including assignment analyses, learning walks, and microteaching. These experiences resulted in a higher degree of teacher credibility with students, not to mention stronger sources of collective teacher efficacy for the team.

The math team, including those who would not be teaching algebra, got down to work. They examined the data currently available to them and listed their strengths and opportunities to grow. In addition, they posed questions about what they wondered.

"So, we agree that we need more formative student assessment data to figure out what our current seventh and eighth graders know," said Mr. McIntyre. "This year's seventh graders will be the first ones affected by the new policy."

"And we want to find out what this year's eighth graders know," Gretchen Reinhart added. "We have some students enrolled in Algebra 1, and others in Pre-Algebra."

Ibrahim Muhammed volunteered, "I'll take this issue to the eighth-grade team. I'd like to get their insights. We'll need their support to implement this well."

Introducing Collective Efficacy in Action.

LISTEN as Doug discusses the collective efficacy cycle and the professional learning cycle, both of which are actions that teams can take related to collective efficacy.

Bethany Carter, who was taking notes for the team, said, "Let's give ourselves two weeks to gather this information. Hopefully we'll be able to settle on a common challenge to guide our work for the next quarter."

Mr. Muhammed nodded in agreement. "I'll echo what Jim said. I'm glad we're in this together."

In this final chapter, we will examine how collective responsibility fosters collective efficacy. We discuss three tools teams can use to move to action: learning walks, microteaching, and assignment analysis. Next, we describe a professional learning cycle template that provides teams with clear steps for systematically engaging in a sequence of actions that promote collective efficacy. We end with four possible starting points for building teacher credibility and collective efficacy at your school.

Collective responsibility fosters collective efficacy.
iStock.com/SDI Productions

Using the "traffic light" scale, identify your systems for collective responsibility. Ask yourself each of these questions:

How well do you know the strengths of the teachers on your team?

How well do you know the strengths of teachers outside of your grade level or subject?

How often do you meet with your team to discuss curriculum, instruction, and assessment?

How often do you meet with other grade levels or departments to discuss curriculum, instruction, and assessment?

How often do colleagues visit your classroom for professional purposes?

How often do you visit your colleagues' classrooms for professional purposes?

ACTION

PAUSE & PONDER

What are you noticing about the patterns in your responses? Are there areas that you'd like to change? As you read this chapter, think about your team as well as other sources of support or learning in your school. Does your team have systems in place to address the needs of all students, and the belief that their efforts will result in amazing learning?

COLLECTIVE RESPONSIBILITY + ACTION = COLLECTIVE EFFICACY

Collective responsibility is foundational for collective efficacy to thrive.

Collective responsibility is defined by Learning Forward across five dimensions (Hirsch, 2010, p. 2):

1. All staff members share a commitment to the success of each student.

2. No single teacher is allowed to fail in her or his attempt to ensure the success of any one student.

3. Our students benefit from the wisdom and expertise of *all* teachers in a grade level or subject, rather than just their own teachers.

4. Our teachers feel a responsibility to share what is working in their classrooms with their colleagues.

5. Teachers with less experience realize that other teachers are invested in their success and the success of all students.

COLLECTIVE RESPONSIBILITY IS FOUNDATIONAL FOR COLLECTIVE EFFICACY TO THRIVE.

If a group does not believe that it is their responsibility to move learning forward, student achievement suffers. In schools where there is a high degree of collective responsibility for academic success and failure, students thrive. You might ask how this would even be possible—don't we all feel responsible for our students' learning? But consider how often you have heard educators blame their students (or their students' families) for not learning. We hear people use poverty, motivation, even screen time as reasons why students don't learn. We are not dismissing these as unimportant. But keep this in mind: Collective teacher efficacy, with an effect size of 1.39, is nearly three times as influential as socioeconomic status (0.52) on student achievement.

REFLECTIVE WRITING

What are the factors of collective responsibility necessary to create collective efficacy?

How is your team positioned for collective responsibility?

What actions are we compelled to take on behalf of students? Use the following planning tool to assist your team in taking action to improve learning for each student.

Goals	Proposed Action	Internal Supports We Will Need	External Supports We Will Need	Date to Revisit (Monitor Progress)
To improve equitable access to content				
To improve teacher clarity				
To improve teacher credibility				
To strengthen expectations				
To remove organizational or institutional barriers				

ACTION

Another threat that undermines collective responsibility is isolating oneself from others. As noted in Chapter 1, the independent contractor and the loner both distance themselves from what is occurring in classrooms outside of their own. Each is concerned only with issues that directly affect him or her, and neither engages in the work of the team to improve learning. That mindset results in the diffusion of responsibility and fosters a false belief that others will take action, so they don't need to. In contrast, all the members of the middle school math team, including those who were not currently teaching algebra, recognized their collective responsibility for math achievement of students at their school. Writers Aminatou Sow and Ann Friedman have their own name for this mutual investment in one another—shine theory: *I don't shine if you don't shine.* In other words, collective responsibility radiates in two directions. The team embraces a belief in its collective responsibility to students and to one another.

Collective Responsibility Is Linked to Achievement

Although the math team in the chapter opening didn't know it at the time, there is a significant positive relationship between high levels of collective responsibility and algebra achievement for eighth and ninth graders, especially boys (Morales-Chicas & Agger, 2017). The researchers examined algebra outcomes using the dataset from the High School Longitudinal Study of 2009 to examine the

SHINE THEORY: I DON'T SHINE IF YOU DON'T SHINE.

association between collective responsibility of teachers and student course grades. They speculate that boys, who have a stronger tendency to attribute their academic achievement to their teachers, are more susceptible to their teachers' sense of responsibility for their learning. Teachers with low collective responsibility are perceived as less credible in the eyes of their students. Morales-Chica and Agger hypothesize that male students "tend to view the teacher as less of a support system and more of a contributor to [their] poor performance in algebra" (p. 67). You will recall that teacher credibility is the perception that a student can learn from a teacher. It is reasonable to believe that students sense when their teachers are not deeply invested in their learning.

Students are sensitive when isolation and lack of collective responsibility are at play in their school. It should not be startling for students to see other teachers regularly in their classrooms. Students should not be surprised that their English teacher is asking them questions about their progress and learning in science. It should be natural for second-grade teachers to refer to discussions with third-grade colleagues when talking with students. Yet in many schools, students rarely witness any signs that teachers collaborate in meaningful ways with one another. In fact, what they may overhear are complaints about professional learning events and how much their teachers dread them. Our students deserve to witness the high-level ways we work together as adults for their benefit, even when students are not on our roster this year.

Collective Efficacy Is Collective Responsibility in Action

Collective responsibility is important, but not sufficient. Without action, collective responsibility devolves to collective guilt. Collective efficacy requires actions that are purposeful and designed to yield results. Teams that enjoy a high degree of collective efficacy are able to set goals for themselves, pursue them, gauge their progress, make changes as needed, and evaluate their impact. When highly efficacious teams proliferate across a school, the organization becomes efficacious. The culture of the school shifts in material ways, and students and families benefit.

When highly efficacious teams proliferate across a school, the culture of the school shifts and students and families benefit.

iStock.com/SDI Productions

Are you wondering about collective efficacy in your school? Use the instrument in Figure 7.1 to start the conversation. The instrument was developed and validated by Tschannen-Moran and Barr (2004) as part of their studies on the relationship between collective teacher efficacy and student achievement. Directions for scoring can be found at https://wmpeople.wm.edu/site/page/mxtsch/researchtools.

Work with your leadership team to administer and analyze the survey. Use the following protocol to link your decisions to your goal of building collective responsibility. Record your own thoughts in advance, and then discuss your ideas with team members.

Question	My Thoughts	Our Collective Thoughts
In what ways has the data collection and analysis process impacted us?		
Do we feel confident that we can meet the needs of our students?		
How will we support the decisions our team has made?		
How might the common challenge change our collective work?		

Figure 7.1 Collective Teacher Beliefs

Collective Teacher Beliefs	This questionnaire is designed to help us gain a better understanding of the kinds of things that create challenges for teachers. Your answers are confidential.								
Directions: **Please indicate your opinion about each of the questions below by marking any one of the nine responses in the columns on the right side, ranging from (1) "None at All" to (9) "A Great Deal" as each represents a degree on the continuum.** **Please respond to each of the questions by considering the** *current* **ability, resources, and opportunity of the teaching staff in your school to do each of the following.**	**None at All**	**Very Little**		**Some Degree**		**Quite a Bit**		**A Great Deal**	
1. How much can teachers in your school do to produce meaningful student learning?	①	②	③	④	⑤	⑥	⑦	⑧	⑨
2. How much can your school do to get students to believe they can do well in schoolwork?	①	②	③	④	⑤	⑥	⑦	⑧	⑨
3. To what extent can teachers in your school make expectations clear about appropriate student behavior?	①	②	③	④	⑤	⑥	⑦	⑧	⑨
4. To what extent can school personnel in your school establish rules and procedures that facilitate learning?	①	②	③	④	⑤	⑥	⑦	⑧	⑨
5. How much can teachers in your school do to help students master complex content?	①	②	③	④	⑤	⑥	⑦	⑧	⑨
6. How much can teachers in your school do to promote deep understanding of academic concepts?	①	②	③	④	⑤	⑥	⑦	⑧	⑨
7. How well can teachers in your school respond to defiant students?	①	②	③	④	⑤	⑥	⑦	⑧	⑨
8. How much can school personnel in your school do to control disruptive behavior?	①	②	③	④	⑤	⑥	⑦	⑧	⑨
9. How much can teachers in your school do to help students think critically?	①	②	③	④	⑤	⑥	⑦	⑧	⑨
10. How well can adults in your school get students to follow school rules?	①	②	③	④	⑤	⑥	⑦	⑧	⑨
11. How much can your school do to foster student creativity?	①	②	③	④	⑤	⑥	⑦	⑧	⑨
12. How much can your school do to help students feel safe while they are at school?	①	②	③	④	⑤	⑥	⑦	⑧	⑨

For office use only.

⓪ ① ② ③ ④ ⑤ ⑥ ⑦ ⑧ ⑨
⓪ ① ② ③ ④ ⑤ ⑥ ⑦ ⑧ ⑨
⓪ ① ② ③ ④ ⑤ ⑥ ⑦ ⑧ ⑨

Tschannen-Moran, M., & Barr, M. (2004). Fostering student learning: The relationship of collective teacher efficacy and student achievement. *Leadership and Policy in Schools*, 3(3), 189–209. Used with permission.

ACTION

SET COLLECTIVE EFFICACY INTO MOTION

Schools are typically organized as teams: the kindergarten team, the social studies team, the intervention team. But these are often in name only, and primarily describe a job function and a list of people to include on group emails. Teams that function with a sense of collective responsibility and efficacy embrace the true intentions of professional learning communities: to work together to investigate challenges that inhibit student learning. Seahorse-Louis and Kruse (1995) note that these are founded on a "process of communicating ideas, ideals, shared concerns, and interests" (p. 216).

WE HAVE WITNESSED THE POWER THAT PROFESSIONAL LEARNING COMMUNITIES CAN HARNESS.

In our work with educators, we have witnessed the power that professional learning communities can harness. The intent, if not the name, can be traced back to Dewey's work in the early part of the last century, and more specifically to school-based curriculum development of the 1970s (see Stoll, Bollam, McMahon, Wallace, & Thomas, 2006, for a systematic review of PLCs). However, the message that instruction is not the concern of the group has produced a gap in the impact of some PLCs. Yet in practice, we see this as an important element of learning. If we accept that curriculum, instruction, and assessment form the triad of learning, why would we deliberately turn away from examining teaching, and the impact of our teaching, as part of our analysis?

As we have argued throughout this book, our credibility and efficacy as teachers is tied in part to our competence as professionals. In that spirit, we developed questions and action tools to guide professional learning communities such that they can examine curriculum, assessment, and instruction (Fisher, Frey, Almarode, Flories, & Nagel, 2019):

1. Where are we going?

2. Where are we now?

3. How do we move learning forward?

4. What did we learn today?

5. Who benefited and who did not benefit?

We hope that you can appreciate the strategic planning baked into the process (Questions 1 and 2), as well as the collective efficacy of providing teams with reflection (Question 4). The fifth question is intended to ensure that issues of equity are fully woven into every conversation. The third question, *How do we move learning forward?* asks teams to put collective efficacy into motion. There are a number of ways to do this, including learning walks, microteaching, and assignment analysis.

THINK ALONG

PLC+. Dominique discusses PLC+ questions that your team can use to collaborate. Does your team regularly discuss instruction and the impact on learning?

How might discussions about instruction strengthen your team's impact?

LEARNING WALKS

Vicarious experiences are a source of collective efficacy, and watching each other in action is one of the best ways to draw from this benefit. Yet for all our good intentions, it is quite difficult to find time to spend in each other's classrooms. Teams benefit from tools that allow them to maximize the supportive structures created to foster collective efficacy (Hord, 1997).

Learning walks are planned and coordinated classroom visits that focus on the common challenge agreed upon by the group.

They have much in common with instructional rounds (City, Elmore, Fiarman, & Teitel, 2009), although they are less formal and more varied. Teaching teams complete a series of short classroom observations (5–10 minutes in length) to gain a sense of the patterns noticed. These are not classroom observations in the conventional sense of the term. First, they are not evaluative. This can be a difficult habit to break, as stating that something is "good" or "effective" is evaluative. Rather, the purpose is to gather objective data focused on a specific common challenge, (e.g., "I noticed that the students in the small group I observed referred to their weekly goals sheets") and then to organize those observations into patterns. See Figure 7.2 for a chart of the types of learning walks and their purposes.

THINK ALONG

Learning Walks. Dominique discusses the value of learning walks. What might you be able to learn from visiting other classrooms? Have you engaged in learning walks?

Figure 7.2 Types of learning walks and their purposes

TYPE OF WALK	PURPOSE	TIME	PARTICIPANTS	FOLLOW UP AFTER THE WALK
Ghost Walk	To examine classrooms without students present. Teachers volunteer to make their classrooms available and in turn are participants in the ghost walk. The focus of the observation is about the physical learning environment.	1 hour	Members of the professional learning community.	*Summary of data collected:* Evidence and wonderings processed within the PLC+ team, or across other professional learning communities.
Capacity-Building Learning Walks	This walk focuses solely on collecting data to inform decisions. Collection of data and evidence help identify the implementation of effective practices and gain insights into next steps.	2 hours	Members of the building leadership team, in partnership with members of the professional learning communities.	*Summary of data collected:* Evidence and wonderings processed within the PLC+ team, or with entire faculty.
Faculty Learning Walks	The goal of this type of learning walk is to focus on the learning of the whole staff. It involves all teachers in visiting other teachers' classroom outside of the PLC+ to which members belong. This can spark new ideas and strategies for teachers to incorporate into their own practice.	All day	Principal, assistant principal, members of the building leadership team, and whoever is available each period and/or time segment, ultimately involving entire faculty throughout the year.	*Summary of data collected:* Evidence and wonderings processed with entire faculty.

Source: Fisher, D., Frey, N., Almarode, J., Flories, K., & Nagel, D. (2019). *The PLC+ playbook: A hands-on guide to collectively improving student learning* (p. 89). Thousand Oaks, CA: Corwin. Used with permission.

Ghost walks are done in the absence of students and are used to focus on the physical environment. For example, a fourth-grade team who has identified academic language use as a common challenge might conduct a ghost walk of each other's classrooms to look for patterns of environmental support for language use. Ghost walks can be conducted virtually using photographs of classrooms. The high school where we work used photographs of posted learning intentions and success criteria to identify trends in purpose and content.

Capacity-building learning walks are conducted within and across teams. The classroom visits are scheduled in advance with volunteer teachers and focus on a specific common challenge. The middle school math team profiled in this chapter used capacity-building learning walks to learn from one another about new ways to foster algebraic thinking. An elementary school with the common challenge of increasing the emotional regulation skills of their students used a series of cross-grade-level capacity-building learning walks to learn about the work of colleagues in this effort with students of different ages.

Instructional leadership teams (ILTs) measure, monitor, and modify professional learning efforts using *faculty learning walks*. Their task is to look for patterns and trends regarding the current focus of the professional learning cycle. These teams are composed of school leaders and teacher leaders who work together to make decisions about the direction of the professional learning. Each professional learning cycle is 10 weeks in length, but this time frame is subject to the findings of these faculty learning walks. It is not uncommon for an ILT to determine that additional learning is warranted, and that the next round of professional learning should be a continuation of the current work and not have an entirely new focus. This decision-making method empowers teachers and school leaders to make evidence-based informed choices about professional learning.

PLANNING FOR LEARNING WALKS IS CRUCIAL.

Planning for Learning Walks Is Crucial

Given that the observations are short, it is important to arrive at an agreed-upon common challenge in advance. Lacking a focus, groups have a tendency to look at everything (and therefore nothing) in an attempt to take in the whole. But a short classroom visit is a snapshot, and nothing more. No one would indiscriminately take a series of photos devoid of any purpose or composition. Wandering in and out of classrooms without a focus is equally unproductive. The planned nature of learning walks means that teachers are able to plan aligned experiences timed to the schedule, thus allowing teams to witness what they came to see.

NOTES

MICROTEACHING

Microteaching is the practice of capturing a portion of a lesson or student interaction on video for the purpose of analyzing it. These are teacher-directed coaching events from inception to discussion with the professional learning community.

The content usually focuses on the common challenge identified by the team. A volunteer teacher uses video capture equipment to record himself, and then views it by himself to identify a segment to take to his team. The volunteer teacher sets the context of the segment for his team and poses his questions. After viewing, the team poses questions meant to mediate the thinking of the volunteer teacher. You will recall from the previous chapter that the questions should not be thinly veiled evaluations or suggestions, but rather be designed to spark the thinking of the volunteer teacher.

INSIDE THE CLASSROOM

Watch teachers engage in microteaching.

What might you be able to learn from microteaching?

Suggested Open-Ended Questions for the Team to Ask the Volunteer Teacher

- What did you want your students to know and be able to do?
- What connections have you made?
- What did you see or hear that confirms your previous thinking?
- What did you see or hear that conflicts with your previous thinking?
- Which moments did you find to be particularly effective?
- Which moments did you think did not go as well as you had hoped?
- What was different in comparing those moments?
- What would you change in order to accomplish your stated goal?
- What do you want to be sure to do again?

(Fisher et al., 2019, p. 98)

Figure 7.3 A comparison of microteaching practices

What Microteaching *Is*		What Microteaching *Is Not*
To co-construct content pedagogical knowledge with the team	*Purpose*	To evaluate someone else's teaching
Identified by the teacher	*Determination of Focus*	Identified by others
Directs the discussion	*Role of the Teacher*	Listens passively
To ask mediating questions to prompt the thinking of the teacher	*Role of Other PLC+ Members*	To provide feedback about the quality of the lesson; to offer judgments and personal opinions

Source: Fisher, D., Frey, N., Almarode, J., Flories, K., & Nagel, D. (2019). *The PLC+ playbook: A hands-on guide to collectively improving student learning* (p. 96). Thousand Oaks, CA: Corwin. Used with permission.

Microteaching, properly implemented, is a significant influencer on student achievement, with an effect size of 0.88 ("250+ Influences," n.d.). It is an effective tool for building teacher credibility for one another, especially as it relates to competence, and can increase the perceived credibility we hold for one another. Perhaps most of all, microteaching fosters collective teacher efficacy through relational trust, vicarious experiences, and social cohesion. See Figure 7.3 for a comparison of what microteaching is and is not.

Microteaching is the practice of capturing a portion of a lesson or student interaction on video for the purpose of analyzing it.

iStock.com/GoodLifeStudio

Use the following microteaching protocol to have productive conversations with your colleagues about the link between teaching and learning.

Before Filming	
What are my goals for this process? (e.g., to improve a teaching technique, to refine my ability to engage in expert noticing, to identify the thinking of a student)	
When and with whom will I need to schedule filming? Who will I need for assistance before, during, or after filming?	
What equipment will I need?	
What do I hope to capture in the video?	
After Filming	
Schedule time to review the footage. In what ways was the lesson you delivered different from the lesson you planned?	
What questions does the video raise for you?	
What questions do you want your team to help you answer?	
In Your Team Meeting	
Introduce the video to your team, set the context, and pose your major questions.	

Suggested questions for team members to ask the teacher:

- What did you want your students to know and be able to do?
- What connections have you made?
- What did you see or hear that confirms your previous thinking?
- What did you see or hear that conflicts with your previous thinking?
- Which moments did you find to be particularly effective?
- Which moments did you think did not go as well as you had hoped?
- What was different in comparing those moments?
- What would you change in order to accomplish your stated goal?
- What do you want to be sure to do again?

Debrief the Microteaching Experience as a Whole	
What did we learn today as a team?	
How might we move student learning forward?	
How might we move our own learning forward?	
What goals do we have for ourselves for the next two weeks?	

ASSIGNMENT ANALYSIS

The third tool in the toolbox for moving learning forward is assignment analysis. This differs from collaborative analysis of student work and from consensus scoring (e.g., Colton, Langer, & Goff, 2015). Both of these practices are quite useful for teams, and there are exceptional protocols for using them. Unlike those approaches, which look at student performance data, assignment analysis is used to design student tasks. Education Trust, a nonprofit organization dedicated to closing opportunity-to-learn gaps in schools, profiled the use of assignment analysis as a means for understanding how rigorously assignments are related to content standards. The rationale is that analysis of assignments provides insight into expectations for students based on what has been taught. Unfortunately, Education Trust's middle school math assignment analysis found that "less than one-third . . . provided an opportunity for students to communicate their thinking or justify their responses" (Education Trust, 2018, p. 4). Similarly, their analysis of middle school literacy assignments found that only 16% required students to "use a text for citing evidence as support for a position or a claim" (Education Trust, 2015, p. 4).

The middle school math team used Education Trust's guidelines to examine their current assignments, in order to increase the opportunities for algebraic thinking. The full math assignment analysis tool is available at https://1k9gl1yevnfp2lpq1dhrqe17-wpengine.netdna-ssl.com/wp-content/uploads/2014/09/Math-Assignment-Analysis-Guide.FINAL-4-18.pdf Based on their findings, they revised some assignments to include this tool.

James McIntyre, the department chair, said,

> It helps us close a loop. We wanted to increase algebraic thinking, and we learned about student think-alouds to help us with that. But it wasn't until we realized that we hadn't created opportunities for them to use think-alouds that we saw the disconnect between our goals and our actions.

His colleagues on the English team used a similar tool to take a closer look at their assignments. (The literacy assignment analysis tool is available at https://edtrust.org/resource/literacy-assignment-analysis-guide/.) During their grade-level professional learning community meetings, math and English colleagues traded information about their findings and subsequent actions. Based on these discussions, they conducted a capacity-building learning walk to learn from one another about their assignment construction efforts.

The three tools introduced in this section are ways for teams to learn from one another together. That said, a jumble of unorganized tools is not likely to result in a lot of productivity. These tools, along with other events inside and outside of your school, should be harnessed so that they can deliver on their full potential. In the following section, we describe a professional learning cycle designed to foster collective efficacy.

A MODEL FOR COLLECTIVE EFFICACY IN ACTION

The middle school math team's willingness and ability to reexamine and improve their practices stems from their school's focus on collective teacher efficacy. They utilized a cycle for professional learning that provides time for teams to learn about, enact, and strengthen their teaching (see Figure 7.4). Their professional learning cycle draws on the research about goal attainment, trust, and knowledge building, as well as other work (DeWitt, 2019; Donohoo, 2013; Knight, 2007), to put collective efficacy in action. These phases contribute to the collective efficacy of the teams as they learn together. As a school community, this process links collective efficacy to what Hoy, Sweetland, and Smith (2002) call "the normative and behavioral environment of the school" (p. 79). The components of this model are not strictly linear. Rather, they are essential habits for moving adult learning forward while building the relational strengths among professional colleagues to take on the work.

REFLECTIVE WRITING

How might the collective efficacy cycle help your team? What goal would you set for yourselves to get started?

Figure 7.4 The professional learning cycle

Identify Common Challenge

Build Knowledge and Skills

Monitor, Measure, Modify Collaborative Planning

Opening Up Practice Collaborative Planning

Safe Practice Collaborative Planning

Identify the Common Challenge

At the risk of stating the obvious, teams perform better when there is a shared goal. Tasks can then be focused on steady progress toward the goal, rather than on filling time but not yielding results. An agreed-upon common challenge is one that is publicly acknowledged, is observable and actionable, and mobilizes teachers to take action (Fisher, Frey, Almarode, Flories, & Nagel, 2019). The math team determined that in order to better identify a common challenge, they would need to gather assessment data. Based on their initial findings, they decided that their common challenge would be to foster algebraic thinking in their seventh- and eighth-grade math classes. They selected this as their common challenge because they wanted to learn about their expectations for their students. The team saw this as exploratory in nature. "We need to find out what works well," explained Ms. Carter.

TEAMS PERFORM BETTER WHEN THERE IS A SHARED GOAL.

Build Knowledge and Skills

New practices are typically introduced through initial professional learning sessions, shared or vicarious experiences, or professional readings. However, the habit of consulting sources to aid in ongoing practice is crucial. The math team met with the district math coach and read several professional papers by mathematics researchers and practitioners. They analyzed current assignments for algebraic thinking opportunities and revised some in order to make tasks more cognitively rigorous.

Use Safe Practice and Collaborative Planning

New professional learning should always include time for teachers to experiment as they take on a new approach.

With two weeks' worth of newly revised lessons in hand, the seventh- and eighth-grade math teachers first tried the lessons out for themselves and shared their early impressions with their colleagues. Over time, they more fully incorporated these approaches into their instructional design.

Open Up Practice and Collaborative Planning

The entire team viewed each other's classrooms to share ideas and observe each other's techniques for incorporating new algebraic thinking approaches into their instruction. Collaborative planning continued, as members traded suggestions and pilot methods. High-functioning teams such as this one regularly open their practice to one another in order to work together systematically and with intention.

THINK ALONG

Safe Practice. Dominique discusses the value of safe practice. Without this, teachers are not likely to innovate. Why is safe practice crucial for building trust and collective efficacy?

Monitor, Measure, and Modify
Through Collaborative Planning

Teams with high collective efficacy appreciate the role each member plays in monitoring for success. Throughout this unit, they will meet regularly to inform one another of what they are witnessing in their own classrooms and adjust as needed. Most of these meetings are not formally scheduled. Rather, they are part of the ongoing professional discussion they hold with one another in the hall, at lunch, and in the parking lot. Imagine how little would be accomplished if we waited until a weekly scheduled meeting to ask each other questions and puzzle over problems. It's likely that little would get done.

This cycle of professional learning is supported by scheduling actions (see Figure 7.5). Each professional learning community at the school posts their learning cycle in the school's professional development room. These publicly posted plans provide other teams with information about what their colleagues are doing, thus reinforcing the normative and behavioral environment of the school that Hoy and colleagues (2002) identified as essential for building collective efficacy. There is something to be said for knowing that the colleagues you see more rarely are similarly engaged in their own professional learning.

Knowing that all the proverbial oars are in the water and rowing in the same direction boosts morale and increases motivation.

REFLECTIVE WRITING

In what ways might publicly posted plans contribute to your knowledge of the strengths of the entire staff? How might this foster collective efficacy?

Figure 7.5 Professional learning cycle for math team

Professional Learning Cycle

Targeted Instructional Area: ___7th and 8th grade Math___   **Practice:** ___   ___Algebraic Thinking___

Cycle # Date Span:	ILT meeting *At least 2 meetings per month* Planning and leading professional learning	Input Training *2-3 meetings per PLC* Professional learning for teachers on how to implement a practice	Safe Practice Teachers experiment with the new practice in a low-risk environment	Professional Reading *At least 4 per PLC* Teachers receive professional articles relevant to the practice being learned	Opening Up Classroom Practice: Peer Observation and Reflection Teachers observe each other and engage in structured reflection/feedback	Collaborative Planning *2 meetings per month: focus on PLC* Teachers look at student work and data	Monitor, Measure, Modify ILT and staff engage in learning walks to look for evidence of implementation
Week 1	School ILT 9/10			Professional reading "Algebra for All" 9/14 PLC+ mtg		9/14 PLC+ mtg (last year's data)	
Week 2		Meet with district math coach 9/18			Assignment Analysis 9/21 PLC+ mtg		
Week 3		District Algebra for All training 9/27		Professional reading on Equitable Algebra 9/28 PLC+mtg		9/28 PLC+ mtg (student examples)	
Week 4	District Math ILT 10/1		10/1-10/5		Ghost walks 10/5 PLC+ mtg		
Week 5			10/8-10/12	Professional reading on student think-alouds 10/12 PLC+mtg		Analyze practice test results 10/12 PLC+ mtg	

(Continued)

Figure 7.5 (Continued)

Cycle # Date Span:	ILT meeting At least 2 meetings per month Planning and leading professional learning	Input Training 2-3 meetings per PLC Professional learning for teachers on how to implement a practice	Safe Practice Teachers experiment with the new practice in a low-risk environment	Professional Reading At least 4 per PLC Teachers receive professional articles relevant to the practice being learned	Opening Up Classroom Practice: Peer Observation and Reflection Teachers observe each other and engage in structured reflection/feedback	Collaborative Planning 2 meetings per month: focus on PLC Teachers look at student work and data	Monitor, Measure, Modify ILT and staff engage in learning walks to look for evidence of implementation
Week 6	School ILT 10/15	District Algebra for All training 10/18			Capacity-building Learning Walks 10/15-10/19		ILT faculty learning walk 10/16
Week 7			10/22-10/26			Look at student exit tickets 10/26 PLC+ meeting	
Week 8			10/29-11/2	Professional reading on Algebra and English learners 11/2 PLC+			
Week 9	District Math ILT 11/5				Micro-teaching 11/9 PLC+ mtg		
Week 10	School ILT 11/12				Capacity-building Learning Walks 11/12-11/16		ILT faculty learning walk 11/14

Adapted from Chula Vista Elementary School District. Cycles of Professional Learning and this planning template developed by Targeted Leadership Consulting. www.targeted leadershipconsulting.net.

You will note in the professional learning cycle developed by the math team that there is mention of ILTs. These instructional leadership teams exist at the school and district levels. District ILTs are formed to focus on specific issues, and most are discipline specific. In this case, the district ILT is for mathematics. In addition, each school has an ILT composed of teacher-leaders representing grade levels and subjects, as well as school administrators, the counselor, social worker, instructional coaches, the English learner coordinator, and special education director. This ILT coordinates efforts at the school level to reduce redundancies and gaps. In this professional learning cycle, the math department joined efforts with the English learner specialists to promote the use of student think-alouds in classes. There are assurances to be derived from coordinated efforts like this. To return to our rowing metaphor for a moment, members of high-performing rowing teams don't waste their energy turning around to make sure the person behind them is doing what is expected.

Teams with high collective efficacy have informal, ongoing professional discussions.
iStock.com/DGLimages

ACTION

LEADERSHIP SUSTAINS COLLECTIVE EFFICACY AND TEACHER CREDIBILITY EFFORTS

The effort to build teacher credibility among students and staff with an eye toward fostering collective teacher efficacy is no small task. It requires sustained and unswerving focus, a willingness to redistribute resources (human and fiscal), and the courage to resist the mission creep that torpedoes so many well-intentioned initiatives.

Build teacher credibility with students by making students an integral part of the process. Student voice can be a powerful motivating factor when students see that their ideas matter. Use tools like the one featured in Chapter 2 on trust, and the one in Chapter 4 on expectancy-value-cost, to start the conversation with students. Their insights are valuable and help all of us continue to strengthen our practices.

Build credibility among the staff by creating opportunities for them to learn from one another. If we are to achieve widespread teacher credibility and collective efficacy, there must be numerous points of contact. Tools such as the immediacy checklist in Chapter 5 aren't worth the paper they are printed on if there is never a chance to use them. The learning walks profiled in this chapter are possible, but only if we agree as a school staff that time spent with colleagues is of the utmost importance.

Examine your own collaborative practices with colleagues as a starting point.

Consider the barriers you directly experience in collaborating with your peers. Individuals need to consider the barriers they have to engaging with peers in productive ways.

PAUSE & PONDER

We ask you, right now, to think about the last time you engaged with your team and to consider each of these statements:

- ☐ It is hard for me to engage with my peers when the project is not my own or at least my own idea.

- ☐ It is hard for me to engage with my peers because I don't feel comfortable sharing my ideas.

- ☐ It is hard for me to engage with my peers because they might not have the same high expectations as I have.

- ☐ It is hard for me to engage with my peers because I am afraid of being wrong or uninformed.

- ☐ It is hard for me to engage with my peers because it is impossible to make everyone happy.

- ☐ It is hard for me to engage with my peers because I avoid conflict.

- ☐ It is hard for me to engage with my peers because I have experienced past failures with group tasks.

ACTION

Your reactions to these reflective statements are real. We don't want to discount or diminish your experiences and feelings. But if any of them are true for you, your ability to impact students' learning using collective teacher efficacy will be compromised. And if your peers are engaged in the same reflective work, you might all just come to realize that we need to put some of our histories aside for the benefits of students.

Support Teacher Leadership Through Disposition and Action

Have you heard of the "tall poppy syndrome"? It is the destructive habit present in too many schools of cutting down peers who appear to elevate their practice. Nothing is served by undermining the efforts and accomplishments of others. Teaching is too difficult without undercutting our collective efforts. If you have a colleague who is great at building trust with students, don't let the fact that you've taught for a decade longer deter you. *Learn from her.* If your strength is in the dynamic way you present information, *be professionally generous*. Encourage younger members of your team to be active on the school's instructional leadership team. Just because you're the grade-level chair doesn't mean you are the only choice. Being a teacher-leader shouldn't be described as *going over to the dark side*. School leaders engage in the hard work of operating the school, leading instruction, and making sure lunch is served each day. They deserve our support and partnership.

Encourage younger members of your team to be active on the school's instructional leadership team.

iStock.com/fizkes

ACTION

Using the "traffic light" scale, identify your systems for collective responsibility. Indicate where your thoughts on peer engagement fall on the scale for each of these statements:

It is hard for me to engage with my peers when the project is not my own or at least my own idea.

It is hard for me to engage with my peers because I don't feel comfortable sharing my ideas.

It is hard for me to engage with my peers because they might not have the same high expectations as I have.

It is hard for me to engage with my peers because I am afraid of being wrong or uninformed.

It is hard for me to engage with my peers because it is impossible to make everyone happy.

It is hard for me to engage with my peers because I avoid conflict.

It is hard for me to engage with my peers because I have experienced past failures with group tasks.

PAUSE & PONDER

CONCLUDING THOUGHTS ABOUT COLLECTIVE EFFICACY IN ACTION

Collective efficacy is a hot topic, again, because of the meta-analysis that Ells (2011) completed that resulted in it being identified as "the new number one" on Hattie's list of influences ("250+ Influences," n.d.). As a result, there are a number of new resources on this topic, and we think it's an important and worthwhile endeavor for schools to pursue. However, in most discussions of collective efficacy, individual teacher credibility is ignored. We think this is a mistake. We see these two constructs feeding on each other. Teams want highly credible members, and strong teams build and reinforce the credibility of teachers with their students. To ignore teacher credibility places collective efficacy at risk.

We also believe that many efforts to build and maintain collective efficacy neglect the communication skills of the adults who are trying to collaborate as well as the processes and vicarious experiences that they can use to build their mastery. We have provided information that teams can use to accomplish both of these things. But honestly, initial efforts will likely include struggle and failures. How teams respond to those struggles will either build or tarnish their collective efficacy. Over time, as teams become more efficacious, they will establish more challenging goals for themselves and their students, and learning will accelerate.

Nancy provides you with a challenge to conclude this chapter. First, what is your role in your school? Are you the loner? The independent contractor? The talker? The amplifier? What can you do to change your credibility and your collective efficacy? How can you support your colleagues?

Nancy's challenge is to improve the collective efficacy of the team and your credibility with students, all in an effort to improve the learning outcomes for your students.

CHAPTER 7 CHALLENGE

What can you do to change your credibility and your collective efficacy?

How can you support your colleagues?

REFERENCES

250+ influences on student achievement. (n.d.) Thousand Oaks, CA: Corwin. Retrieved from https://us.corwin.com/sites/default/files/250_influences_chart_june_2019.pdf

Adams, C. M., & Forsyth, P. B. (2009). Conceptualizing and validating a measure of student trust. *Studies in School Improvement, 47*, 263–279.

Allensworth, E., Ponisciak, S., & Mazzeo, C. (2009). *The schools teachers leave: Teacher mobility in Chicago public schools.* Chicago: Consortium on Chicago School Research.

Andersen, J. A. (1979). Teacher immediacy as a predictor of teaching effectiveness. In B. D. Ruben (Ed.), *Annals of the International Communication Association Yearbook* (Vol. *3*, pp. 543–559). Brunswick, NJ: Transaction Books.

Baier, A. C. (1994). *Moral prejudices: Essays on ethics.* Cambridge, MA: Harvard University Press.

Bandura, A. (1993). Perceived self-efficacy in cognitive development and functioning. *Educational Psychologist, 28*, 117–148.

Bandura, A. (1997). *Self-efficacy: The exercise of control.* New York: W. H. Freeman.

Banfield, S. R., Richmond, V. P., & McCroskey, J. C. (2006). The effect of teacher misbehaviors on teacher credibility and affect for the teacher. *Communication Education, 55*(1), 63–72.

Baringer, D. K., & McCroskey, J. C. (2000). Immediacy in the classroom: Student immediacy. *Communication Education, 49*(2), 178–186.

Barsade, S. G., Ward, A. J., Turner, J. D. F., & Sonnenfeld, J. A. (2000). To your heart's content: A model of affective diversity in top management teams. *Administrative Science Quarterly, 45*(4), 802–836.

Brown, B. (2012). *Daring greatly: How the courage to be vulnerable transforms the way we live, love, parent, and lead.* New York: Gotham.

Bryk, A., & Schneider, B. (2003). Trust in schools: A core resource for reform. *Educational Leadership, 60*(6), 40–45.

Bryk, A., Sebring, P., Allensworth, E., Luppescu, S., & Easton, J. (2010). *Organizing schools for improvement: Lessons from Chicago.* Chicago: University of Chicago Press.

Carver-Thomas, D., & Darling-Hammond, L. (2017). *Teacher turnover: Why it matters and what we can do about it.* Palo Alto, CA: Learning Policy Institute.

Castek, J., Henry, L., Coiro, J., Leu, D., & Hartman, D. (2015). Research on instruction and assessment in the new literacies of online research and comprehension. In S. Parris & K. Headley (Eds.), *Comprehension instruction: Research-based best practices* (3rd ed., pp. 324–344). New York: Guilford.

City, E. A., Elmore, R. F., Fiarman, S. E., & Teitel, L. (2009). *Instructional rounds in education: A network approach to improving teaching and learning.* Cambridge, MA: Harvard Education Press.

Collier, L. (2015, June). Grabbing students: Researchers have identified easy ways to boost student success by increasing their engagement in learning. *Monitor on Psychology, 46*(6). Retrieved from https://www.apa.org/monitor/2015/06/grabbing-students

Colton, A., Langer, G., & Goff, L. (2015). *Collaborative analysis of student learning: Professional learning that promotes success for all.* Thousand Oaks, CA: Corwin.

Costa, A. L., & Garmston, R. J. (2015). *Cognitive coaching: Developing self-directed leaders and learners* (3rd ed.). Lanham, MD: Rowman & Littlefield.

Covey, S. (2008). *The speed of trust: The one thing that changes everything*. New York: Simon & Schuster.

Daane, M. C., Campbell, J. R., Grigg, W. S., Goodman, M. J., & Oranje, A. (2005). Fourth-grade students reading aloud: NAEP 2002 special study of oral reading. *The Nation's Report Card*. NCES 2006-469. Washington, DC: National Center for Education Statistics.

DeWitt, P. (2019). How collective teacher efficacy develops. *Educational Leadership, 76*(9), 31–35.

Donohoo, J. (2013). *Collaborative inquiry for educators. A facilitator's guide to school improvement*. Thousand Oaks, CA: Corwin.

Duke, N. K., & Pearson, P. D. (2002). Effective practices for developing reading comprehension. In A. E. Farstrup & S. J. Samuels (Eds.), *What research has to say about reading instruction* (3rd ed., pp. 205–242). Newark, DE: International Reading Association.

Education Trust. (2015). *Checking in: Do classroom assignments reflect today's higher standards?* Retrieved from https://edtrust.org/resource/classroomassignments/

Education Trust. (2018). *Checking in: Are math assignments measuring up?* Retrieved from https://edtrust.org/resource/checking-in-are-math-assignments-measuring-up/

Ells, R. J. (2011). *Meta-analysis of the relationship between collective teacher efficacy and student achievement*. Unpublished doctoral dissertation. Chicago: Loyola University of Chicago.

Fisher, D., Frey, N., Almarode, J., Flories, K., & Nagel, D. (2019). *PLC+: Better decisions and greater impact by design*. Thousand Oaks, CA: Corwin.

Fisher, D., Frey, N., Amador, O., & Assof, J. (2018). *The teacher clarity playbook*. Thousand Oaks, CA: Corwin.

Fisher, D., Frey, N., & Hattie, J. (2016). *Visible learning in literacy*. Thousand Oaks, CA: Corwin.

Frymier, A. B., & Thompson, C. A. (1992). Perceived teacher affinity-seeking in relation to perceived teacher credibility. *Communication Education, 41*, 388–399.

Fuller, B., Waite, A., & Irribarra, D. T. (2016). Explaining teacher turnover: School cohesion and intrinsic motivation in Los Angeles. *American Journal of Education, 122*, 537–567.

Goddard, R., Goddard, Y., Kim, E. S., & Miller, R. (2015). A theoretical and empirical analysis of the roles of instructional leadership, teacher collaboration, and collective efficacy beliefs in support of student learning. *American Journal of Education, 121*(4), 501–530.

Good, T. L. (1987). Two decades of research on teacher expectations. *Journal of Teacher Education, 38*, 32–47.

Good, T. L., & Lavigne. A. L. (2018). *Looking in classrooms* (11th ed.). New York: Routledge.

Good, T. L., Sterzinger, N., & Lavigne. A. L. (2018). Expectation effects: Pygmalion and the initial 20 years of research. *Educational Research and Evaluation, 24*(3–5), 99–123.

Graves, M. F., & Fitzgerald, J. (2003). Scaffolding reading experiences for multilingual classrooms. In G. G. García (Ed.), *English learners: Reaching the highest level of English literacy* (pp. 96–124). Newark, DE: International Reading Association.

Hattie, J. (2009). *Visible learning: A synthesis of 800 meta-analyses relating to achievement*. New York: Routledge.

Hattie, J. (2019.) https://visible-learning.org/hattie-ranking-influences-effect-sizes-learning-achievement/]

Herrera, T. (2019, February 3). Do you keep a failure résumé? Here's why you should start. *New York Times*. Retrieved from https://www.nytimes.com/2019/02/03/smarter-living/failure-resume.html

Hess, J. A. (n.d.). *Effective instructional practices: Optimizing your immediacy*. Washington, DC: National Communication Association. Retrieved November 16, 2019, from https://www.natcom.org/sites/default/files/pages/EIP_Optimizing_Your_Immediacy.pdf

Hirsch, S. (2010). Collective responsibility makes all teachers the best. *Teachers Teaching Teachers*. Retrieved from https://learningforward.org/docs/leading-teacher/sept10_hirsh.pdf?sfvrsn=2

Hord, S. M. (1997). *Professional learning communities: Communities of continuous inquiry and improvement*. Austin, TX: Southwest Educational Development Laboratory.

Hoy, W. K., Sweetland, S. W., & Smith, P. A. (2002). Toward an organizational model of achievement in high schools: The significance of collective efficacy. *Education Administration Quarterly, 38*(1), 77–93.

Hoy, W. K., & Tschannen-Moran, M. (2003). The conceptualization and measurement of faculty trust in schools: The omnibus T-Scale. In W. K. Hoy & C. G. Miskel (Eds.), *Studies in leading and organizing schools* (181–208). Greenwich, CT: Information Age.

Hudson, R. F., Lane, H. B., & Pullen, P. C. (2005). Reading fluency assessment and instruction: What, why, and how? *Reading Teacher, 58*(8), 702–714.

Hurk, H., Houtveen, A., & Grift, W. (2017). Does teachers' pedagogical content knowledge affect their fluency instruction? *Reading & Writing, 30*(6), 1231–1249.

Jenkins, L. (2015). *Optimize your school: It's all about the strategy*. Alexandria, VA: ASCD.

Kelly, S., Rice, C., Wyatt, B., Ducking, J., & Denton, Z. (2015). Teacher immediacy and decreased student quantitative reasoning anxiety: The mediating effect of perception. *Communication Education, 64*(2), 171–186.

Knight, J. (2007). *Instructional coaching: A partnership approach to improving instruction*. Thousand Oaks, CA: Corwin.

Levin, S., & Bradley, K. (2019). *Understanding and addressing principal turnover: A review of the research*. Reston, VA: National Association of Secondary School Principals.

Los Angeles County Office of Education. (2002). *TESA teacher handbook* (Updated). Los Angeles, CA: Author.

Marinak, B. A., & Gambrell, L. B. (2016). *No more reading for junk: Best practices for motivating readers*. Portsmouth, NH: Heinemann.

Marzano, R. J. (2011). Relating to students: It's what you do that counts. *Educational Leadership, 68*(6), 82–83.

McCroskey, J. C., & Young, T. J. (1981). Ethos and credibility: The construct and its measurement after three decades. *Communication Studies, 32*, 24–34.

Mehrabian, A. (1971). *Silent messages*. Belmont, CA: Wadsworth.

Morales-Chicas, J., & Agger, C. (2017). The effects of teacher collective responsibility on the mathematics achievement of students who repeat algebra. *Journal of Urban Mathematics Education, 10*(1), 52–73.

Newberry, M., Sanchez, L. O., & Clark, S. K. (2018). Interactional dimensions of teacher change: A case study of the evolution of professional and personal relationships. *Teacher Education Quarterly, 45*(4), 29–50.

Ormond, T., & Kiechle, M. (1999). Teacher's proximity to "problem students" and its effect on academic learning time in physical education. *Research Quarterly for Exercise and Sport, 70*(1), A97.

Palmer, P. (1998). *The courage to teach*. San Francisco, CA: Jossey-Bass.

Pearson, P. D., & Gallagher, G. (1983). The gradual release of responsibility model of instruction. *Contemporary Educational Psychology, 8*, 112–123.

Quaglia, R., & Corso, M. (2014). *Student voice: The instrument of change*. Thousand Oaks, CA: Corwin.

Reid, L. W., & Pell, C. (2015). Communities and crime. In J. D. Wright (Ed.), *International encyclopedia of social and behavioral sciences* (2nd ed., pp. 322–327). New York: Elsevier.

Reina, D. S., & Reina, M. L. (2010). *Rebuilding trust in the workplace*. San Francisco, CA: Berrett–Koehler.

Remillard, J. T., Baker, J. Y., Steele, M. D., Hoe, N. D., & Traynor, A. (2017). Universal Algebra 1 policy, access, and inequality: Findings from a national survey. *Education Policy Analysis Archives, 25*(101/102), 1–25.

Reynolds, G. (2008). *Presentation Zen: Simple ideas on presentation design and delivery*. Berkeley, CA: New Riders.

Richmond, V. P., McCroskey, J. C., & Johnson, A. D. (2003). Development of the nonverbal immediacy scale (NIS): Measures of self- and other-perceived nonverbal immediacy. *Communication Quarterly, 51*(4), 504–517.

Santa, C., & Havens, L. (1995). *Creating independence through student–owned strategies: Project CRISS*. Dubuque, IA: Kendall-Hunt.

Seahorse-Louis, K., & Kruse, S. D. (1995). Getting there: Promoting professional community in urban schools. In K. Seahorse-Louis & S. D. Kruse (Eds.), *Professionalism and community: Perspectives on reforming urban schools* (pp. 208–227). Thousand Oaks, CA: Corwin.

Senge, P., Cambron-McCabe, N., Lucas, T., Smith, B., & Dutton, J. (2012). *Schools that learn: A fifth discipline fieldbook for educators, parents, and everyone who cares about education* (2nd ed.). New York: Crown Business.

Shapiro, S. (2007). Revisiting the teachers' lounge: Reflections on emotional experiences and teacher identity. *Teaching and Teacher Identity, 6*, 616–621.

Shulman, L. S. (1986). Those who understand: Knowledge growth in teaching. *Educational Researcher, 15*, 4–14.

Sills-Briegel, T. (1996). Teacher-student proximity and interactions in a computer laboratory and classroom. *Clearing House, 70*(1), 21–23.

Southerland, S., & Gess-Newsome, J. (1999). Preservice teachers' views of inclusive science teaching as shaped by images of teaching, learning, and knowledge. *Science Education, 83*(2), 131–150.

Stanley, D. (2003). What do we know about social cohesion? The research perspective of the federal government's social cohesion research network. *Canadian Journal of Sociology, 28*(1), 5–17.

Stoll, L., Bollam, R., McMahon, A., Wallace, M., & Thomas, S. (2006). Professional learning communities: A review of the literature. *Journal of Educational Change, 7*, 221–258.

Tate, M. (2015). Worksheets don't grow dendrites: 20 instructional strategies that engage the brain (3rd ed.). Thousand Oaks, CA: Corwin.

Tobin, K. (1987). The role of wait time in higher cognitive level learning. *Review of Educational Research, 57*(1), 69– 95.

Tschannen–Moran, M., & Barr, M. (2004). Fostering student learning: The relationship of collective teacher efficacy and student achievement. *Leadership and Policy in Schools, 3*(3), 189–209.

Tschannen–Moran, M., & Hoy, W. (1998). A conceptual and empirical analysis of trust in schools. *Journal of Educational Administration, 36*, 334–352.

Velez, J. J., & Cano, J. (2008). The relationship between teacher immediacy and student motivation. *Journal of Agricultural Education, 49*(3), 76–86.

von Frank, V. (2010). Trust matters—for educators, parents, and students. *Tools for Schools, 14*(1), 1–3.

Wangberg, J. K. (1996). Teaching with a passion. *American Entomologist, 42*(4), 199–200.

Ward, P., & Ayvazo, S. (2016). Pedagogical content knowledge: Conceptions and findings in physical education. *Journal of Teaching in Physical Education, 35*(3), 194–207.

Wigfield, A., & Eccles, J. S. (2000). Expectancy-value theory of achievement motivation. *Contemporary Educational Psychology, 25*(1), 68–81.

Zeiger, S. (2018, June 18). *List of core competencies for educators*. Retrieved from https://work.chron.com/list-core-competencies-educators-8916.html

INDEX

CORWIN HAS ONE MISSION: to enhance education through intentional professional learning.

We build long-term relationships with our authors, educators, clients, and associations who partner with us to develop and continuously improve the best evidence-based practices that establish and support lifelong learning.